CONTENTS

Ships in Focus Publications

Correspondence and editorial:
Roy Fenton
18 Durrington Avenue
London SW20 8NT
020 8879 3527
rfenton@rfenton.demon.co.uk
Orders and photographic:
John & Marion Clarkson
18 Franklands, Longton
Preston PR4 5PD
01772 612855
sales@shipsinfocus.co.uk

Printed by Amadeus Press Ltd.,
Cleckheaton, Yorkshire.
Designed by Hugh Smallwood,
John Clarkson and Roy Fenton.
SHIPS IN FOCUS RECORD
ISBN 1 901703 15 0

SHIPS IN FOCU

The colour section in *Record*
by regular readers. The exp
and in order to maximise it:
unusual split of one article. ... ...
mention of two people whose extreme helpfulness made
colour possible, Jim McFaul, custodian of the World Ship
Photo Library's slide collection, and Ian Farquhar.

Observant regulars will note that we have not
designated one feature as 'Fleet in Focus' in this issue,
although both Paul Boot's Bank Line opus and the article on
the PLM colliers could merit the title. But fear not,
devotees, the feature will return with a vengeance in the
next issue, when John B. Hill covers the post-war *Granges*
of Houlder Brothers. We have plans for this feature for over
a year ahead, but suggestions are welcome and will be
heeded, like that of the reader who reminded us that we have
neglected the Ellerman group, an omission we will
endeavour to make good.

No *Record* editorial would be complete without a
reminder to subscribers, and we make no apology for this:
any specialist periodical like *Record* depends utterly on a
high proportion of readers taking out and regularly
renewing their subs. Remember, you are keeping us afloat
and cutting yourself a good deal, especially if you go for
six- or nine-issue subscriptions.

John Clarkson   Roy Fenton
October 2001

SUBSCRIPTION RATES FOR RECORD

Subscribers make a saving on postage, and receive each *Record* just as
soon as it is published. They are also eligible for concessions on
newly-published *Ships in Focus* titles. Readers can start their
subscription with *any* issue, and are welcome to backdate it to receive
previous issues.

	3 issues	6 issues	9 issues
UK	£23	£44	£63
Europe (airmail)	£25	£47	£68
Rest of world (surface mail)	£25	£47	£68
Rest of world (airmail)	£30	£56	£81

Gowanbank was the 54th and last motorship to be built by Harland and Wolff for
Bank Line. Sold along with her sister *Maplebank* to Gourdomichalis-managed
companies in 1979, she went to the breakers six years later as *Kavo Grossos*.
See pages 110 to 121.   *[Airfoto/Paul Boot collection]*

THE PLM COLLIERS 12 TO 27
Roy Fenton

Colliers from the Tees

The end of the First World War saw the PLM determined to continue running the fleet it had built up during hostilities, probably encouraged by the high freight rates which persisted for several years. Indeed, the railway made a substantial investment in purpose-built and technically-sophisticated tonnage. Two groups of ships were ordered from British yards, although with the clamour for ships at this time delivery did not begin until the end of 1920. As discussed in the first part of this article, the PLM ships were registered under the name of the Société Nationale d'Affretèments

Although later in numerical order, the group of larger ships emerged first. Known as 'les grands PLMs', the eight ships numbered *PLM 20* to *PLM 27* were built by Sir Raylton Dixon and Co. Ltd. at Middlesbrough. Technically they were most interesting, demonstrating that companies whose main business is not in shipping may well be in the van of innovation in ship design. The most striking feature of these engines-aft colliers was their steel hatch covers, and whilst the contemporary shipping press did not claim that they were the first ships to be so fitted, they must have been amongst the pioneers. Certainly such hatches were all but unknown amongst contemporary British-owned colliers. The quadruple expansion engines chosen were also unusual for ships of such a size, this type usually being reserved for higher-powered machinery intended for ships large enough to show a worthwhile saving from an additional, fourth expansion of the steam.

The smaller ships *PLM 12* to *PLM 17*, and inevitably known as 'les petits PLMs', began to be delivered from Smith's Dock Co. Ltd., Middlesbrough in January 1921. They lacked the steel hatch covers of the larger ships and had conventional triple expansion machinery by the builders. Both groups of ships were coal-fired.

As the new ships were delivered, the ships of the rather motley wartime fleet were sold off, although the *PLM 8* forestalled her sale when she was wrecked on the Portugese coast in 1922. By 1925 all that remained was the *PLM 10*, one of the oldest wartime acquisitions, which was not sold until 1928.

The PLMs' trade

In post-war years, the PLMs continued to load coal at English and Welsh ports, as well as at Dunkirk and Rotterdam. At the last-named it was transhipped in the Waalhaven from barges which had brought it from Germany. It would be difficult to find a more roundabout route for getting coal from the Rhine valley to southern France, and the long voyage from northern European ports to the Mediterranean was economical only with a paying return cargo. Therefore, after unloading at Port de Bouc, near Marseilles, the PLM ships would drop down to North Africa to load a cargo of bauxite for northern Europe. One other cargo for which the larger ships' steel hatch covers made them particularly suitable was railway rolling stock, and several photographs show them with such a load.

Despite nationalisation of the French railways in 1937, when the PLM became part of the Société Nationale des Chemins de Fer (SNCF), the pattern of trade of the PLM ships continued more or less unbroken, even beyond the outbreak of the war in 1939. However, the Second World War was to scatter the fleet widely, and at one time ships of the fleet were serving on two sides, or perhaps three if the ambiguous nature of the Vichy French is taken into account.

February 1940 saw *PLM 15* and *PLM 25* torpedoed and mined respectively, with considerable loss of life. Following the fall of France in summer 1940, the ships in U.K. ports - *PLM 14, PLM 17, PLM 22* and *PLM 27* - were requisitioned by the British Government and assigned to British managers. To these were added *PLM 13* and *PLM 21* which had remained under Vichy French control but were captured by the British in 1941 and 1942. They were to prove useful ships to a hard-pressed Britain, whether on the east coast carrying coal or loading ore in West Africa or in the Maritimes. Indeed, it was considered worth re-engining *PLM 14* late in 1941. Losses were heavy, however, and if *PLM 14* is included, four out of the six under British control suffered major casualties. The loss of *PLM 27* was particularly unfortunate - and possibly avoidable. By taking advantage of shore searchlights which illuminated the targets at regular intervals, *U 518*

made a surface attack on ore-laden ships anchored off Wabana, Newfoundland. *Rose Castle* (7,803/1915) was also lost in the same attack, which suggests that the defenders had not learned their lesson, as just two months earlier *Saganaga* (5,484/1935) and *Lord Strathcona* (7,335/1915) had been sunk in similar fashion.

Despite this attrition rate, those which served the Allied cause were the lucky ones. *PLM 20*, which remained under the French flag, was torpedoed by a British submarine in 1942. None of the five ships requisitioned by the Germans on or after the fall of France was still afloat at the end of hostilities, although *PLM 26* was later raised, only to be broken up without returning to service.

Of the fleet of 14 ships, all that remained to be returned to their owners at the end of the war were *PLM 13*, *PLM 14* and *PLM 17*. They were put back into service, but within six years all were sold and were not replaced. All traded for up to ten years further for their new owners, and surprisingly it was the ship which had been re-engined in 1941 which went for scrap first, the others lasting until their fortieth birthdays in 1961.

The trade of the PLM ships was certainly an unusual one, and there can be no more eloquent testimony to the economics of sea transport than a railway company carrying its own coal between - amongst others - domestic ports in ships.

Three views of PLMs at war. Opposite is *PLM 13*, or *PLM XIII* according to the nameboard on her bridge, in Ministry of War Transport service photographed in New York harbour by the United States Coastguard on 17th October 1942. She survived the war to have the longest life of any PLM collier. [Courtesy Bill Schell]

The top photograph on this page was taken with an extreme telephoto lens by German military intelligence from Algeciras in 1943, and shows one of the larger PLMs in Gibraltar, although the British battleship in the background is probably the reason for the Abwehr's interest. If the date is correct it can only be the ill-fated *PLM 21*, which was captured by the Allies in Algeria late in 1942, but came to grief off South Wales in 1944. [Peter Newall collection]

The middle photograph shows *Paula*, ex-*PLM 12*, under Allied attack. *Paula* was sunk by the British 8th Destroyer Flotilla on 17th September 1943, in the rather chaotic situation which followed the surrender of Italy. The German forces in Greece were desperately trying to reinforce various islands in the Aegean which had been garrisoned by Italians. The Royal Navy waded in, in this instance attacking a convoy which included *Paula* and *Pluto*. It is tempting to believe this shows *Paula's* final moments, but the viewpoint suggests it was taken not from a destroyer but from an aircraft. [Sammlung Siersdorfer 150/59, courtesy George Scott]

This page bottom: a peacetime view of *PLM 14* as *Larrivet*, owned in Bordeaux from 1953 to 1959.[Fotoflite incorporating Skyfotos, courtesy George Scott]

11. PLM 12 1921-1943

3,442g 2,084n 345.0 x 49.5 x 25.0 feet
T. 3-cyl. by Smith's Dock Co. Ltd., Middlesbrough; 430 NHP, 9 knots.

19.7.1920: Launched by Smith's Dock Co. Ltd., Middlesbrough (Yard No.760).

1.1921: Completed for Société Nationale d'Affrêtements, Paris, France as PLM 12.

13.4.1943: Taken over by Germany at Marseille, operated by Mittelmeer Reederei GmbH, Berlin and renamed PAULA.

17.9.1943: Sunk by the British destroyers HMS FAULKNOR and HMS ECLIPSE north of Stampalia in the Dodecanese.

A trials view of *PLM 12*. [Redcar and Cleveland Museums Service]

12. PLM 13 1921-1951

O.N. 174321 3,442g 2,084n 345.0 x 49.5 x 25.0 feet
T. 3-cyl. by Smith's Dock Co. Ltd., Middlesbrough; 430 NHP, 9 knots.

13.10.1920: Launched by Smith's Dock Co. Ltd., Middlesbrough (Yard No.761).

4.1921: Completed for Société Nationale d'Affrêtements, Paris, France as PLM 13.

18.2.1941: Intercepted by the Ocean Boarding Vessel HMS MARSDALE (4,890/1940) in position 28.12 north by 12.23 west and taken to Gibraltar.

12.3.1941: Registered in the ownership of the Ministry of Shipping, London.

9.5.1941: Christian Salvesen and Co., Leith, appointed managers.

8.1941: Owners became the the Ministry of War Transport, London.

16.7.1945: UK register closed on return to French Government.

1946: Owners became Société Nationale des Chemins de Fer Francais (Société Nationale d'Affrêtements, managers), Paris.

1951: Sold to W. Rostedt, Abo, Finland and renamed MARIANNE.

1958: Sold to the Three Diamonds Shipping Corporation, Monrovia, Liberia (Eugenia Saridis and Constantinos Bastas) and renamed DIMITRAKIS.

28.2.1961: Laid up at Piraeus.

20.3.1961: Breaking up began at Perama.

13. PLM 14 1921-1951

O.N. 167029 3,442g 2,084n 345.0 x 49.5 x 25.0 feet
T. 3-cyl. by Smith's Dock Co. Ltd., Middlesbrough; 424 NHP, 10 knots.

12.1941: Fitted with new T. 3-cyl. engines by John Brown and Co. Ltd., Clydebank; 447 NHP, 2,100 BHP, 2,325 IHP, 11½ knots.

9.2.1921: Launched by Smith's Dock Co. Ltd., Middlesbrough (Yard No.762).

6.1921: Completed for Société Nationale d'Affrêtements, Paris, France as PLM 14.

17.7.1940: Taken over by the UK at Methil

15.8.1940: Registered in the ownership of the Ministry of Shipping, London (Christian Salvesen and Co., Leith, managers).

17.10.1940: Damaged by E-boat in position 52.52 north by 02.06 east whilst on a voyage from London to the Tyne in ballast and abandoned. Ten of the crew were lost.

18.10.1940: Taken in tow by HMS MALCOLM and HMS WYVERN and beached on Haile Sands the next day.

20.10.1940: Refloated and taken to Immingham.

8.1941: Owners became the Ministry of War Transport, London.

27.11.1945: UK register closed on return to French Government.

PLM 13 in the colours of Société Nationale des Chemins de Fer. [World Ship Photo Library Brownell collection]

PLM 14 probably in a British coal port. [F.W. Hawks collection]

PLM 14 as *Protee* of Société Navale Caennaise. [W.H.Brown, World Ship Photo Library Brownell collection]

PLM 15. [Collection of Dr. Paul Bois]

1946: Owners became Société Nationale des Chemins de Fer Francais (Société Nationale d'Affrêtements, managers), Paris.
1951: Sold to Société Navale Caennaise (Anciennement G. Lamy et Compagnie, managers), Caen, France and renamed PROTEE.
1953: Sold to Compagnie Maritime et Commerciale du Sud-Ouest, Bordeaux, France and renamed LARRIVET.
10.11.1959: Arrived at La Seyne to be broken up by Société de Material Naval du Midi.
1.12.1959: Breaking up began.

14. PLM 15 1921-1940
4,016g 2,081n 345.0 x 49.5 x 25.0 feet
T. 3-cyl. by Smith's Dock Co. Ltd., Middlesbrough; 430 NHP, 9 knots.
7.6.1921: Launched by Smith's Dock Co. Ltd., Middlesbrough (Yard No.763).
10.1921: Completed for Société Nationale d'Affrêtements, Paris, France as PLM 15.
18.2.1940: Torpedoed and sunk by the German submarine U 37 in position 43.37 north by 09.15 west whilst on a voyage from Oran in convoy 10 RS. Her entire crew was lost.

Right: *PLM 16* in a French port sometime after the outbreak of war: she appears to be in grey. *[Captain J.F. van Puyvelde]*

Below right: *PLM 17. [Peter Newall collection]*

Bottom: *PLM 20* from a vignetted original. *[Captain J.F. van Puyvelde]*

15. PLM 16 1921-1942

4,005g 2,075n 345.0 x 49.5 x 25.0 feet
T. 3-cyl. by Smith's Dock Co. Ltd., Middlesbrough; 430 NHP, 9 knots.
3.10.1921: Launched by Smith's Dock Co. Ltd., Middlesbrough (Yard No.764).
12.1921: Completed for Société Nationale d'Affrêtements, Paris, France as PLM 16.
18.12.1942: Taken over by Germany and operated by Mittelmeer Reederei GmbH, Berlin under the names ELBE and PETER.
23.9.1944: Sunk five miles north of Skiathos in the Gulf of Volos in the Aegean by HM Submarine VAMPIRE.

16. PLM 17 1921-1950

O.N. 167804 4,008g 2,073n 345.0 x 49.5 x 25.0 feet
T. 3-cyl. by Smith's Dock Co. Ltd., Middlesbrough; 430 NHP, 11 knots.
3.10.1921: Launched by Smith's Dock Co. Ltd., Middlesbrough (Yard No.765).
2.1922: Completed for Société Nationale d'Affrêtements, Paris, France as PLM 17.
17.7.1940: Taken over by the UK at Methil.
12.8.1940: Registered in the ownership of the Ministry of Shipping, London (Evan Thomas Radcliffe and Co., Cardiff, managers).
8.1941: Owners became the Ministry of War Transport, London.

4.9.1945: UK register closed on return to French Government.
1946: Owners became Société Nationale des Chemins de Fer Francais (Société Nationale d'Affrêtements, managers), Paris.
1950: Sold to Donati e figli e A. Malli, Trieste, Italy and renamed BRUCIATUTTO.
1953: Owners became Malli e Donati Navegazione Societa a.v.c., Trieste and renamed MADO.
1954: Sold to Cornigliano Societa per Azioni, Genoa, Italy and renamed SIDEROS.
1958: Managers became Sidermar S.p.A.
4.1961: Breaking up began by ARDEM at Vado Ligure.

As discussed in the text, the PLMs occasionally carried cargoes of rolling stock on their steel hatch covers. *PLM 21* is seen with a deck cargo of freight cars, possibly bound for Algeria. *[Collection of Captain J.F. van Puyvelde]*

17. PLM 20 1920-1942
4865g 3007n 414.0 x 56.0 x 28.4 feet
Q. 4-cyl. by the North Eastern Marine Engineering Co. Ltd., Wallsend-on-Tyne; 529 NHP.
3.6.1920: Launched by Sir Raylton Dixon and Co. Ltd., Middlesbrough (Yard No.621).
12.1920: Completed for Société Nationale d'Affrètements, Paris, France as PLM 20.
1.3.1942: Torpedoed and sunk by HM Submarine UNBEATEN five miles east of Mehedia, Tunisia whilst on a voyage from Sfax to Tunis with a cargo of phosphate.

18. PLM 21 1921-1942
5,529g 2,784n 414.0 x 56.0 x 28.4 feet
Q. 4-cyl. by the North Eastern Marine Engineering Co. Ltd., Wallsend-on-Tyne; 529 NHP.
31.8.1920: Launched by Sir Raylton Dixon and Co. Ltd., Middlesbrough (Yard No.622).
2.1921: Completed for Société Nationale d'Affrètements, Paris, France as PLM 21.
11.11.1942: Taken over by Allied forces at Skikda, Philippeville, Algeria.
3.12.1944: Sank after striking Middle Channel Rocks off Milford Haven whilst on a voyage from Newport with a cargo of coal.

19. PLM 22 1921-1940
O.N. 165787 5,529g 2,784n 414.0 x 56.0 x 28.4 feet
Q. 4-cyl. by the North Eastern Marine Engineering Co. Ltd., Wallsend-on-Tyne; 529 NHP, 2,600 IHP, 11 knots.
28.10.1920: Launched by Sir Raylton Dixon and Co. Ltd., Middlesbrough (Yard No.623).
4.1921: Completed for Société Nationale d'Affrètements, Paris, France as PLM 22.
4.7.1940: Placed under armed guard in the Tyne.
17.7.1940: Taken over by the UK on the Tyne.
24.7.1940: Registered in the ownership of the Ministry of Shipping, London (William A. Carr, Newcastle-on-Tyne, manager).
27.8.1940: Manager became Trevor L. Price, Cardiff.
27.6.1941: Torpedoed and sunk by the German submarine U 123 south west of the Canary Isles in position 25.43 north by 22.47 west whilst on a voyage from Pepel, Sierra Leone to the Tees with a cargo of ore in convoy SL 76. Of the complement of 43, which included two French navy gunners and one passenger, 32 were lost.
16.8.1941: Register closed.

PLM 22. Ships *PLM 22* to *PLM 25* had modified cargo gear compared with *PLM 20* and *PLM 21*. *[F.W. Hawks collection]*

20. PLM 23 1921-1940

5,529g 2,784n 414.0 x 56.0 x 28.4 feet
Q. 4-cyl. by the North Eastern Marine Engineering Co.
Ltd., Wallsend-on-Tyne; 529 NHP.
23.12.1920: Launched by Sir Raylton Dixon and Co. Ltd.,
Middlesbrough (Yard No.624).
6.1921: Completed for Société Nationale d'Affrêtements,
Paris, France as PLM 23.
4.8.1940: Taken over at Bordeaux by the German
Government, Berlin, Germany (Reederei Unterweser A.G.,
Bremen, Germany, managers). Given the number R1N, and
later A1N for Operation Seelowe.
29.12.1940: Wrecked in position 53.58.04 north by 08.17
east of Scharhorn.

21. PLM 24 1921-1942

5,461g 2,711n 414.0 x 56.0 x 28.4 feet
Q. 4-cyl. by Richardsons, Westgarth and Co. Ltd.,
Middlesbrough; 532 NHP.
5.9.1921: Launched by Sir Raylton Dixon and Co. Ltd.,
Middlesbrough (Yard No.626).
12.1921: Completed for Société Nationale d'Affrêtements,
Paris, France as PLM 24.
17.12.1942: Taken over at Port de Bouc by Germany and
operated by Mittelmeer Reederei GmbH, Berlin. One
source has her renamed PERIGORD.
7.9.1943: Mined and sunk in the Aegean in position 39.22
north by 23.25 east with a cargo of ammunition.

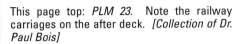

This page top: *PLM 23.* Note the railway
carriages on the after deck. *[Collection of Dr.
Paul Bois]*

This page middle: *PLM 24. [Collection of Dr.
Paul Bois]*

This page bottom: *PLM 25* arriving light ship,
probably at a British coal port. Note the
derricks from the kingposts stowed up against
the mainmast. *[F.W. Hawks collection]*

Opposite upper: *PLM 26* had further modified
cargo gear, with very long derricks, here seen
stowed up against the masts. She appears to
be in a dark over all colour scheme.

Opposite bottom: *PLM 27* at Doel on the River
Scheldt in 1936. *[Captain J.F. van Puyvelde]*

22. PLM 25   1922-1940

5,461g 2,711n 414.0 x 56.0 x 28.4 feet
Q. 4-cyl. by Richardsons, Westgarth and Co. Ltd., Middlesbrough; 532 NHP.
31.10.1921: Launched by Sir Raylton Dixon and Co. Ltd., Middlesbrough (Yard No.627).
3.1922: Completed for Société Nationale d'Affrêtements, Paris, France as PLM 25.
27.2.1940: Mined and sunk five miles from the Cromer Knoll Lightvessel in position 53.19 north by 01.12 east whilst on a voyage from the Tyne to St. Nazaire. Four of her crew were lost.

23. PLM 26   1922-1940

5,461g 2,711n 414.0 x 56.0 x 28.4 feet
Q. 4-cyl. by Richardsons, Westgarth and Co. Ltd., Middlesbrough; 532 NHP.
13.12.1921: Launched by Sir Raylton Dixon and Co. Ltd., Middlesbrough (Yard No.628).
4.1922: Completed for Société Nationale d'Affrêtements, Paris, France as PLM 26.
4.8.1940: Taken over by German forces at Bordeaux and renamed OSTFRIESLAND. Given the number R2N, and later A2N for Operation Seelowe.
12.5.1941: Sunk by Allied aircraft at Hamburg.
30.5.1941: Refloated.
8.1941: Owners Admiral der Kriegesmarinediestele, Berlin, Germany (Fisser und van Doornum, Emden, Germany, managers), and renamed OSTFRIESLAND.
15.10.1944: Caught fire after being attacked by Allied

aircraft at Wilhelmshafen.
30.3.1945: Sunk by Allied aircraft at Wilhelmshafen.
2.3.1946: Refloated.
26.7.1946: Left in tow of tugs SALVONIA and EMPIRE MARY for St. Nazaire.
11.6.1947: In course of demolition by Société Nazairienne de Démolitions. She was stripped at Penhoet Docks and towed to Coueron for demolition.

24. PLM 27   1922-1940

O.N. 165979 5,461g 2,711n 414.0 x 56.0 x 28.4 feet
Q. 4-cyl. by Richardsons, Westgarth and Co. Ltd., Middlesbrough; 532 NHP.
2.3.1922: Launched by Sir Raylton Dixon and Co. Ltd., Middlesbrough (Yard No.629).
7.1922: Completed for Société Nationale d'Affrêtements, Paris, France as PLM 27.
17.7.1940: Taken over by the UK at Glasgow
31.7.1940: Registered in the ownership of the Ministry of Shipping, London (Gibbs and Co., managers, Cardiff).
8.1941: Owners became the Ministry of War Transport, London.
2.11.1942: Torpedoed and sunk by the German submarine U 518 whilst anchored off Wabana, Bell Island, Newfoundland in position 47.36 north by 52.58 west whilst on a voyage from Wabana to Sydney, Nova Scotia with a cargo of iron ore for the Dominion Steel and Coal Corporation Ltd. Of the crew of 43 and six gunners, 12 of the crew were lost.
18.11.1942: Register closed.

HERRING AND CAVIAR TO CANADA
Peter Newall

Captain (later Sir) William Petersen (1856-1925) was a shipping entrepreneur who tried to break the hold of the conference lines to Canada but was never successful in his numerous attempts to enter the market. This is the story of Petersen's efforts to break into the trade and the subsequent success of his initiatives under the ownership of the Canadian Northern Railway.

Proving the turret

Little is known of Petersen's early life apart from the fact that he was born at St. Jorgensberg, Denmark and at one time held a commission in the Danish Navy. In 1884 he was given his first command of a British cargo ship, *Augusta* (902/1872). In 1891 he went into partnership with Arthur Tate and formed the Newcastle-based Petersen, Tate and Co. The company's first ship was *Guildford* (2,281/1882) and her master was Captain Petersen. In May of the following year, the Turret Steam Shipping Co. Ltd. was founded as a joint venture between Petersen, Tate and Co. and the shipbuilder William Doxford and Sons to own and operate the first Doxford turret ship, *Turret* (1,970/1882). Managed by Petersen, Tate and Co., the engines-aft prototype *Turret* was viewed with great suspicion by the shipping community, especially underwriters who refused to provide insurance cover. Objections were soon dispelled after Captain Petersen took the revolutionary vessel on its first voyage and, despite heavy weather, the ship performed well. As the advantages of the turret ship became apparent, orders started to flow into the yard and it became one of the most successful and well-known standard types with 182 built between 1892 and 1911.

Petersen, Tate and Co. owned or managed nine turret ships and from 1893 most were used to carry coal between Sydney, Nova Scotia and Montreal for the Dominion Coal Company and the turret was a familiar sight on the St. Lawrence River and in the Great Lakes.

Breaking into the Canadian passenger trade

Captain Petersen also appears to have made friends with senior Canadian politicians especially those in the Liberal Party, which came to power in 1896. Under the leadership of Wilfred Laurier, Prime Minister until 1911, the Liberals were responsible for the settlement of over a million people into Manitoba and the western territories of Saskatchewan and Alberta. In March 1897 Petersen's company was offered the contract for a subsidised, fast passenger-mail service between Canada and Liverpool using four 20-knot, 10,000gt ships based on the turret design. Hawthorn Leslie and Co. agreed to build the three-funnelled ships. Unfortunately, Petersen was unable to find sufficient finance to fund the scheme and so a year later the offer was withdrawn causing great embarrassment for the Liberal Government.

Undaunted by this setback, William Petersen apparently tried to buy Beaver Line which was sold to Elder, Dempster in 1899. In 1900, Arthur Tate resigned and a new firm was formed in 1901, W. Petersen Ltd. Also in 1901 the Sydney to Montreal coal contract appears to have been awarded to the newly-formed Canadian Ocean and Inland Navigation Co. Ltd. of Toronto, founded by William Mackenzie and Donald Mann. Mackenzie and Mann were a dynamic duo involved in a number of Canadian transport ventures, the principal of which was the Canadian Northern Railway which developed a 3,000-mile transcontinental railway, completed in 1915, in competition with the Canadian Pacific and Grand Trunk Railways. Canadian Ocean and Inland bought the five remaining turret ships from Petersen although he continued to manage the vessels until 1904. Between 1903 and 1904, W. Petersen also managed three British-built engines-aft Great Lakes ships *A.E. Ames* (1,637/1903), *H.M. Pellatt* (1,591/1903) and *J.H. Plummer* (1,582/1903). These interesting ships were ordered by another Mackenzie and Mann controlled company, Canadian Lake and Ocean Navigation Co. Ltd.

In 1900 one of Petersen's companies, Northern Transport Ltd., and its three ships was bought by Owen Philipps and later transferred to King Line. This was the first shipping line acquired by the young Welshman, later Lord Kylsant, and was the start of an ambitious take-over programme which would ultimately lead to the establishment of one of the largest British shipping empires.

1904 saw Petersen involved in yet another attempt to break into the Canadian passenger market. This time, the ships were two former Royal Mail Steam Packet Company liners, *Minho* and *Ebro* (both 3,377/1896), which were part of a trio built by Napier and Sons principally for an emigrant service to South America. The two vessels were purchased in November 1903 by Henry Swan (of Swan Hunter) and were renamed respectively *Halifax* and *Quebec* in May 1904. Managed by W. Petersen Ltd., the two ships started an emigrant service between Rotterdam and Canada but, after a few voyages during the summer months, they were laid up in the Tyne and sold to French Line in February 1905. It is unclear if this venture was the one referred to in Petersen's obituary as follows: 'He then had another attempt at running a service to Canada with a subsidy from the Canadian Government, but this resulted in heavy losses.' With no more ships to manage, the ever-resourceful Petersen turned his attention to the development of another controversial cargo ship design, this time with a corrugated hull, and in June 1905 he

An artists impression of a turret-hulled passenger ship planned by Petersen in 1897. *[Courtesy John Lingwood]*

became a founding partner in the Monitor Shipping Corporation Ltd.

New York and Continental

In 1907 a new cargo service, the New York and Continental Line, was established by Robertson, Shankland and Co., London to carry grain from New York to Hamburg and Rotterdam using chartered tonnage. The grain arrived at New York in trains operated by the Erie Railroad Company which ran between Chicago and New York and it is likely that the railway company had a stake in the new firm. One of the principals of the New York and Continental, Robert Shankland of Greenock, was also the owner of the Burn Line and two of his ships, *Otterburn* and *Springburn*, were chartered between September 1907 and January 1908.

In early 1908 New York and Continental Line

decided to operate an emigrant service between Rotterdam, Halifax and New York and in mid-March bought two elderly British India Line sisters, *Jelunga* and *Avoca*. The inaugural sailing from Rotterdam took place a week later on 21st March using the chartered *Volturno*. The use of *Volturno* was significant as this ship was associated with the Canadian Northern Railway and was originally registered under the management of Harry William Harding, a name which is often linked with Canadian Northern. The next departure from Rotterdam was *Avoca* and this was a disastrous voyage with a breakdown outbound and a serious collision in the New Waterway on the return voyage which resulted in the ship being towed to Rotterdam for repairs. Worse was to follow with passenger loads significantly lower than expected and the service ceased in August. *Avoca* was subsequently arrested whilst *Jelunga* was returned to British India Line.

Towards the end of the 19th century, Denny of Dumbarton built a trio of passenger liners for British India Associated Steamers. Designed for the British India service to Queensland, they also had temporary accommodation for emigrants in the 'tween decks. The first of the sisters *Jumna* was scrapped in 1907 after use as a pilgrim carrier to Mecca. A year later, the remaining pair, *Avoca* (top photograph) and *Jelunga* (middle), despite being 'hot weather' ships, were given a new lease of life as transAtlantic emigrant carriers for the newly-formed New York and Continental Line. With accommodation altered to take 1,000 in steerage, on April Fools' Day 1908 *Avoca* set off from Rotterdam on her first and only voyage for her new owners. This ended disastrously after a late arrival at Halifax with a broken main steam pipe and a collision with a German steamer on her return to the New Waterway. *Jelunga* managed three voyages before the company folded and she was handed back to British India. Her final days were spent in Hong Kong where she was wrecked in a typhoon in 1923. *Avoca* meanwhile was sold in 1909 to the Uranium Steamship Co. Ltd. and renamed *Uranium*. As such she was chartered to the North-West Transport Line which took over New York and Continental's Rotterdam emigrant service. A year later, with Canadian Northern Steamships' management, a new line was established under the Uranium Steamship banner. In January 1913 *Uranium* ran aground near Halifax whilst going to the rescue of Allan Line's *Carthaginian* which was on fire - fortunately she was refloated soon afterwards (bottom). Three years later she and the rest of the Canadian Northern fleet were sold to Cunard Line and, as *Feltria*, her luck finally ran out on 5th May 1917 when she was torpedoed and sunk in the Atlantic. A further photo of *Avoca* as a Boer War hospital ship can be found on page 113 of *Record* 10. *[All: Peter Newall collection]*

In its year of operation, North-West Transport chartered a number of interesting vessels for the emigrant run to Canada and the United States. Among these was the twelve-year old former Castle Line *Raglan Castle* (top) which had a life almost as varied as *Avoca* - they were also both in the Danish East Asiatic fleet in 1907. One of a pair designed for the Castle Line intermediate service, she was sold in 1904 by the Union-Castle Mail Steamship Co. Ltd. to Barclay, Curle in part payment for new ships. Her period with North-West Transport lasted from March to July 1909. In 1911 she became a whale factory ship, a career which lasted until her demolition at Rosyth in 1934. She can be seen as *Ready* on page 160 of *Record* 7.

In 1888 Mala Real Portuguesa (Portuguese Royal Mail) was formed to operate a subsidised monthly passenger-mail line to the Portuguese African colonies of Moçambique and Angola. Four handsome ships with clipper stems, *Rei de Portugal, Malange, Loanda* and *Moçambique*, were ordered from the Greenock shipyard, Scott and Co. Unfortunately, the service, which operated via Suez, was too ambitious and, within a few years, the company went bankrupt. In 1898, Mala Real was reformed to provide a passenger-mail service to South America using *Rei de Portugal, Malange*, and *Moçambique* - the last mentioned was renamed *Alvares Cabral* after the Portuguese discoverer of Brazil. This too ended in failure and in 1902 *Rei de Portugal* and *Alvares Cabral* were sold to Prince Line as *Napolitan Prince* and *Sicilian Prince* for its Italy to New York emigrant service. Despite being British, Prince Line had been carrying passengers to the United States from Italy since the 1890s and built up a sizeable trade in emigrants. By 1906 the company landed almost 16,000 passengers at New York and this growth led to the order for three twin-funnelled ships from James Laing, Sunderland. Because of increased competition from Italian lines, however, this trio was sold on the stocks to the newly formed Lloyd Sabaudo and by 1908 Prince Line withdrew from the trade. Surplus to requirements, *Napolitan Prince* (middle) and *Sicilian Prince* (bottom) were chartered to North-West Transport for four round voyages each to New York. Sold in 1911, they both survived the war and were sold for scrap in the late 1920s. *[Middle: World Ship photo Library; bottom: Peter Newall collection]*

North-West Transport Line

The failure of New York and Continental provided William Petersen with his third opportunity to enter the North American passenger business and in January 1909 he announced the formation of the North-West Transport Line which would provide a regular fast passenger-cargo service between Hamburg, Rotterdam and New York, with an outbound call at Halifax to land passengers. Although Petersen was the manager of the fortnightly service, the financial backing almost certainly came from the Canadian Northern Railway which was interested in attracting emigrants to land close to its railway line. The principal vessels used in the operation, *Volturno* and the former *Avoca* now renamed *Uranium*, were owned by single ship companies controlled by Canadian Northern. These two were supplemented by four interesting chartered vessels: Prince Line's *Napolitan Prince* and *Sicilian Prince*, a former Castle liner *Raglan Castle* and an Italian emigrant carrier *Campania*.

Although the first sailing was in February 1909, the fortnightly service started in April with Rotterdam the main port of departure. Within a relatively short period, westbound passenger numbers were about 500 per month and in August North-West Transport announced that it had bought two crack passenger ships *Cairo* and *Heliopolis* from the shipbuilder Fairfield which had repossessed the ships after the failure of the Egyptian Mail Steamship Co. This pair would be used across the Atlantic in summer and in the Mediterranean during the winter months. However, the plan was changed following the formation by Canadian Northern Railway on 2nd October of the Toronto-based Canadian Northern Steamships Limited.

After much speculation, William Mackenzie and Donald Mann revealed their hand early in 1910 when it was announced that the purchaser of *Cairo* and *Heliopolis* was, in fact, Canadian Northern Steamships. A new company was set up called The Royal Line which would offer a fortnightly passenger-mail service between Bristol and Canada in direct competition with Canadian Pacific's Liverpool service. *Cairo* and *Heliopolis* were renamed respectively *Royal Edward* and *Royal George* whilst *Volturno*, which had also been transferred to Canadian Northern ownership, was intended to be renamed *Royal Sovereign*.

Designed for the Italian emigrant trade, of all the ships on the Rotterdam-Halifax-New York emigrant service, *Volturno* appears to have had the earliest connection with the Canadian Northern Railway. This small vessel also carried over a thousand emigrants and inaugurated the passenger services for each of the three emigrant lines: New York and Continental in 1908, North-West Transport in 1909 and Uranium in 1910.

On 9th October 1913 disaster struck in mid-Atlantic when she caught fire en route to New York with 657 passengers and crew. Her lethal cargo of chemicals and inflammable materials exploded and the resulting conflagration meant that the large number of passenger ships which came to her rescue had to standby unable to help - the first on the scene was Cunard Line's *Carmania* from where the photographs were taken. Only after oil was poured on the water by the tanker *Narragansett* (see *Record* 16) could the rescue proceed. Unfortunately most of the 136 lives lost were in lifeboats which either capsized or were lost in the heavy swell. *[Top: Martin Lindenborn collection; middle and bottom: Peter Newall collection]*

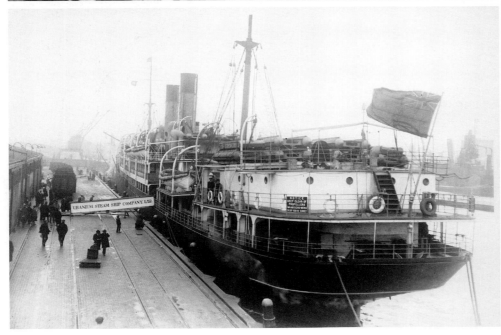

Lloyd Sabaudo Soc. Anon. di Nav. was founded in Turin in June 1906 with the backing of the Royal House of Savoy, hence the name of the company and royal names of its first three ships which were originally ordered by Prince Line: *Re d'Italia, Regina d'Italia* and *Principe di Piemonte*. Despite these grand names, they were principally emigrant carriers with space for 1,900 in steerage. In 1914 *Principe di Piemonte* was bought by Canadian Northern Steamships as a replacement for the lost *Volturno*. Interestingly, the money from the sale was used to place an order with the Glasgow builder, William Beardmore, for a magnificent new liner, *Conte Rosso*. Although this ship became the aircraft carrier *Argus*, in the 1920s Beardmores built a series of ships for the company with *Conte* names, which were among the finest Italian passenger ships of all time. Renamed *Principello* (top), she only made five return voyages from Rotterdam before being transferred to the Avonmouth to Montreal service. The Dutch photographer, Cornelis Nieuwland (1882-1966), had a contract with Uranium Line and took many excellent photographs of the ships in the fleet, including those of emigrants on board (left) and of the officers of *Principello* (opposite). Note also the numerous life rafts on the stern view at Rotterdam (bottom). In 1916 *Principello* was sold to Cunard as *Folia* and was sunk by a German submarine in the Atlantic on 11th March 1917. *[All: Martin Lindenborn]*

Royal and Uranium Lines

In the end, Canadian Northern decided to operate two separate lines. The top end of the market, the caviar eaters, would be served by Royal Line with its passenger terminal at Avonmouth and direct links to London via the Great Western Railway. Although some steerage passengers would travel from Avonmouth, the principal emigrant service continued from Rotterdam under the banner of the Uranium Steamship Co. Ltd. with Canadian Northern Steamships the managers. Having lost the management contract, William Petersen later tried unsuccessfully to obtain a 'finder's fee' for the purchase of *Cairo* and *Heliopolis*.

The only ship owned by the Uranium Steamship Co. Ltd. was *Uranium*. The remainder of the fleet, *Volturno* and *Campanello*, although owned by Canadian Northern, were in fact chartered by Uranium Line. *Volturno* was not transferred to Royal Line and took the first sailing from Rotterdam in April 1910. The same vessel had also inaugurated the services of the two previous incarnations, the New York and Continental and North-West Transport Lines. In its first year of operation, Uranium Line carried over 6,000 passengers westbound and by 1912 this figure had grown to almost 28,000. The following year was an 'annus horribilis' for the company with the grounding of *Uranium* near Halifax in January and the terrible fire mid-Atlantic in October which destroyed *Volturno* with the loss of 136 lives. In 1914 *Principello* was bought as a replacement for *Volturno* whilst the Russian-flagged but Canadian Northern-owned *Ekaterina* entered service as an emigrant feedership between the Baltic and Rotterdam. Many of the Uranium Line passengers were Russian Jews and a favourite item on the menu was undoubtedly pickled herring.

Uranium Line also operated a small feedership which carried emigrants, mainly Russian Jews, from the Baltic to Rotterdam. Registered at Riga in 1914, *Ekaterina* was completed for the General Steam Navigation Co. Ltd. only two years earlier as the short sea cargo-passenger ship *Mavis*. In September 1913 she collided in the New Waterway with the German *Colmar* in thick fog. One passenger was killed in his cabin and the ship sank. She was later raised and sold by General Steam who appear to have been so ashamed of the episode that she is not listed in the fleet lists in either of the official company histories.

During the war *Ekaterina* was requisitioned by the Russian Navy and at war's end became part of the Russian Government merchant fleet. As *Frants Mering*, she was only deleted from *Lloyd's Register* in 1960 although she was probably disposed of some time earlier.

Note the name *Ekaterina* in English and Cyrillic in the photo showing her maiden arrival at Rotterdam. [*Martin Lindenborn*]

Royal Line also started with a flourish and by the end of its first season in 1910 it had not only broken the Canadian transAtlantic record but also carried over 13,000 passengers. In October both ships were registered in Toronto as a sop to growing Canadian nationalism. By 1913 the Royal Line name was dropped in favour of Canadian Northern Steamships. The company's fortune changed, however, with the outbreak of war in 1914 when both *Royal Edward* and *Royal George* were requisitioned as troop transports and the service was operated by *Uranium, Principello* and *Campanello*. For the parent company, Canadian Northern Railway, the boom years of the early 1900s were over and its financial situation had become very precarious. By now, Cunard Line had become active on the Canadian scene with the purchase of Thomson Line and the controlling interest in Anchor Line, which later operated a joint service to Canada with Donaldson Line. *Royal Edward* was sunk by a U-boat in 1915 and the following year Canadian Northern with all its ships and goodwill was sold to Cunard. In 1917 Canadian Northern Railway was nationalised by the Canadian Government and became part of the new Canadian National Railway Company in 1918.

By the war's end, only *Royal George* survived out of the four ships sold to Cunard. The three emigrant carriers had each been given an 'F' name ending in 'ia' by Cunard but were all sunk by submarine attack. Captain Petersen meanwhile had prospered and by 1914 had a large fleet of cargo ships, many with *Rio* names, carrying coal to South America. Unfortunately, his war losses were great with eleven of his fleet sunk by enemy submarines. In 1917, he bought the Island of Eigg as his Scottish retreat and in 1920 he was knighted.

When the Liberal Party returned to power in Canada during the early 1920s under the premiership of William Mackenzie King, Petersen put forward a proposal to the Canadian Government for a subsidised cargo service between Europe and Canada which would significantly undercut the rates agreed by the conference lines on the route. Ten ships with corrugated hulls were to be built with passenger accommodation and refrigerated space. On the strength of the negotiations with the government, two ships, *River Ottawa* and *River St. Lawrence*, were ordered from D. and W. Henderson on the Clyde but, once again, there was a public outcry and Petersen was summoned to Ottawa. As he was preparing to meet Prime Minister Mackenzie King, Sir William collapsed and died on 12th June 1925. With his death the scheme was abandoned and the two extraordinary-looking ships were bought on the stocks by King Line and completed as *King James* (5,066/1925) and *King Malcolm* (5,064/1925) respectively (see *Record* 1, page 47). The latter remained in service until 1960 whilst the final turret ship, *Nuestra Señora del Carmen* (3,482/1895), was wrecked three years later in 1963 by which time, the name of the pioneer Danish captain had long since been forgotten.

The well-known Italian line, Navigazione Generale Italiana, also purchased a trio of British-built ships, *British Princess, British Prince* and *British Empire,* for the Genoa to New York emigrant trade. These large four-masted cargo ships with 'tween deck space for troops or emigrants were built at the turn of the century by Palmers for the Liverpool-based British Shipowners' Co. Ltd., which was founded in 1864. The three operated on the Phoenix Line's Antwerp to New York service and were sold to Navigazione Generale Italiana following the liquidation of British Shipowners' in 1906. The former *British Empire* became *Campania* and like her sisters was converted to carry over 2,000 passengers in steerage class. In February 1910, she was chartered by North-West Transport but was bought later that year by Canadian Northern and renamed *Campanello,* presumably because of confusion with Cunard Line's *Campania.* Sold with the rest of the fleet to Cunard in 1916, as *Flavia* on 24th August 1918 she too was torpedoed and sunk by a German U-boat. *[Martin Lindenborn]*

The magnificent *Cairo* and *Heliopolis* were built on the Clyde by Fairfield for the Egyptian Mail Steamship Company's fast service from Marseilles to Alexandria. By a strange co-incidence the yard number for *Volturno* (448) was just before that of *Heliopolis* (449). These ships were turbine driven with triple screws and capable of over 20 knots. The accommodation for first class passengers was also of a high standard and received very positive comment. The planned volume of traffic did not materialise, however, and by the beginning of 1909 Egyptian Mail was liquidated and the ships repossessed by the shipbuilder. In 1910, they were bought by Canadian Northern Steamships for a new passenger-mail service between Avonmouth and Canada. Modified for Atlantic service and renamed respectively *Royal Edward* (above) and *Royal George* (below) they commenced operations for Royal Line in May 1910. Despite unsubstantiated comments about their rolling in rough weather, they broke the Canadian transAtlantic record and carried substantial numbers of passengers. In 1914 both ships were requisitioned as troop transports and the following year on 13th August *Royal Edward* was sunk by a German submarine in the Mediterranean with great loss of life. Although *Royal George* became part of the Cunard fleet in 1916, her name remained unchanged, possibly in deference to the reigning British monarch. After the war, she was used initially on the Liverpool to New York route and later on the Southampton to New York service. In 1922 she was scrapped at Wilhelmshafen. *[Both: Peter Newall collection]*

The "Royal George" at Avonmouth.

List of vessels owned or chartered for passenger services to Canada and the USA

1. VOLTURNO 1906-1913

O.N. 123737 3,586g 2,284n 340.0 x 43 x 20.7 feet
T. 3-cyl. by the Fairfield Shipbuilding and Engineering Co. Ltd., Govan driving twin screws; 450 HP, 2,750 IHP, 14 knots. 24 cabin and 1,090 third class passengers.
5.9.1906: Launched by the Fairfield Shipbuilding and Engineering Co. Ltd., Govan (Yard No. 448) for Navigazione Italo-Americana, Naples as VOLTURNO.
11.11.1906: Sold to the Volturno Steam Ship Co. Ltd. (H.W. Harding, manager), London.
3.1908: Chartered to the New York and Continental Line for a Rotterdam-Halifax-New York passenger service.
2.1909: Chartered to North-West Transport Line for a Rotterdam-Halifax-New York passenger service.
30.3.1910: Acquired by Canadian Northern Steamships Ltd., Toronto. Intended to be used for the Royal Line Avonmouth-Montreal service as ROYAL SOVEREIGN but chartered to Uranium Steam Ship Co. Ltd. for a Rotterdam-Halifax-New York passenger service.
9.10.1913: Destroyed by fire in position 48.49 north by 34.39 west whilst on a voyage from Rotterdam to New York. Of the 564 passengers and 93 crew, 136 lost their lives.

2. PRINCIPELLO 1914-1916

O.N. 136640 5,365g 4,040n 430.0 x 52.7 x 25 feet
T. 3-cyl. by George Clark Ltd., Sunderland driving twin screws; 869 HP, 5,500 IHP,14.5 knots
120 first and 1,700 third class passengers.
1914: 60 second, 1,900 third passengers.
28.2.1907: Launched by Sir James Laing and Sons Ltd., Sunderland (Yard No. 623) for Lloyd Sabaudo Soc. Anon. di Nav., Genoa as PRINCIPE DI PIEMONTE.
One of a trio ordered for Prince Line but bought whilst on the stocks for a Genoa-New York passenger service.
6.1907: Completed.
1.1914: Acquired by Canadian Northern Steamships Ltd., Toronto as a replacement for VOLTURNO.
12.2.1914: Registered in the ownership of the Principello Steamships Ltd., Toronto (H.W. Harding, London, manager) as PRINCIPELLO.
Chartered to the Uranium Steam Ship Co. Ltd. for a Rotterdam-Halifax-New York passenger service.
10.1914: Transferred with CAMPANELLO to the Royal Line's Avonmouth-Montreal service as replacements for ROYAL GEORGE and ROYAL EDWARD which had become troopships.
17.5.1916: Sold to the Cunard Steam Ship Co. Ltd., Liverpool and later renamed FOLIA.
11.3.1917: Torpedoed by the German submarine U 53 four miles east south east of Ram Head, County Waterford in position 51.51 north by 07.41 west whilst on a voyage from New York to Avonmouth with general cargo. Twelve lives were lost.

3. CAMPANIA/CAMPANELLO 1910-1916

O.N. 115224 9,285g 5,839n 470.0 x 56.8 x 32.1 feet
T. 3-cyl. by Palmers' Shipbuilding and Iron Co. Ltd., Jarrow driving twin screws; 800 HP, 4,400 IHP, 12.25 knots
29.8.1901: Launched by Palmers' Shipbuilding and Iron Co. Ltd., Jarrow (Yard No. 755).
One of a trio of cargo ships with 'tween-deck space for emigrants or troops.
31.10.1901: Registered in the ownership of the British Shipowners' Co. Ltd., Liverpool as BRITISH EMPIRE. Operated for the Phoenix Line on an Antwerp-New York service.
5.1906: On the liquidation of British Shipowners' Co. Ltd., sold to Navigazione Generale Italiana, Genoa and renamed CAMPANIA.
1907: Fitted with accommodation for 90 cabin and 2,200 third class passengers by Cantieri Navali Riuniti, Genoa.
3.1907: Placed on a Genoa-New York service.
1910: Sold to Canadian Northern Steamships Ltd., Toronto.
4.1910: Began operating under the British flag for the Rotterdam-Halifax-New York passenger service of Uranium Steam Ship Co. Ltd. as CAMPANIA.
16.9.1910: Registered in the ownership of H. W. Harding (Company Secretary of Canadian Northern Steamships Ltd.), London and renamed CAMPANELLO.
10.1914: Transferred to Royal Line's Avonmouth-Montreal service.
28.4.1915: Owners became Campanello Steamships Ltd. (Canadian Northern Steamships Ltd.), Toronto.
20.5.1916: Sold to the Cunard Steam Ship Co. Ltd., Liverpool and later renamed FLAVIA.
24.8.1918: Torpedoed and sunk by the German submarine U 107 north west by west of Tory Island in position 55.23 north by 09.40 west whilst on a voyage from Montreal to Avonmouth with general cargo and horses. One life was lost.

4. URANIUM 1908-1916

O.N. 98663 5,324g 3,410n 420.0 x 48.2 x 30.6 feet
Q. 4-cyl. by William Denny and Co., Dumbarton; 627 HP, 4,680 IHP, 13 knots (trial speed 15.5 knots)
80 first, 42 second, and 400 third class passengers.
9.6.1891: Launched by William Denny and Brothers, Dumbarton (Yard No. 448).
20.8.1891: Registered in the ownership of British India Associated Steamers Ltd., Glasgow as AVOCA.
8.1895: Bareboat charter to Compañía Trasatlántica, Barcelona as troopship to Cuba. Registered in Spain as SAN FERNANDO.
6.1897: Returned to British India Associated Steamers Ltd., Glasgow and reverted to AVOCA.
7.1903: Owners became British India Steam Navigation Co. Ltd., London.
29.5.1907: Sold to A/S Det Østasiatiske Kompagni (East Asiatic Co.), Copenhagen and renamed ATLANTA.
3.1908: Sold to Robertson, Shankland and Co. Ltd., London for the New York and Continental Line's Rotterdam-Halifax-New York emigrant service. Accommodation modified to: 80 first, 1,000 third class passengers. Renamed AVOCA.
17.5.1908: Whilst on a voyage from the Hook of Holland to Hamburg collided in fog in the New Waterway with the German steamer NORDSEE (4,439/1907) which sank about three miles off the Hook of Holland with the loss of two lives including the pilot. AVOCA was badly damaged and L. Smit and Sons was engaged to salvage her.

Volturno (left). *[Peter Newall collection]*

Uranium with black funnel between 1910-1914 (opposite upper) and with yellow funnel with black top after 1914 (opposite lower). *[Both: Martin Lindenborn collection]*

8.1908: Arrested at Rotterdam.

11.1908: Sold at auction to C. G. Ashdown and Co.

2.1909: Sold to Uranium Steam Ship Co. Ltd., London and renamed URANIUM. Manager was William Petersen whilst mortgagee was William Mackenzie of the Canadian Northern Railway. Operated a Rotterdam-Halifax-New York service for North-West Transport Line.

4.1910: Rotterdam-Halifax-New York service now operated under the title of Uranium Steam Ship Co. Ltd.

6.1910: Manager became to H. W. Harding, Company Secretary of Canadian Northern Steamships Ltd.

12.1.1913: Aground at Chebucto Head, near Halifax. Later refloated.

9.1914: Sold to Canadian Northern Steamships Ltd., Toronto.

20.5.1916: Sold to the Cunard Steam Ship Co. Ltd., Liverpool and later renamed FELTRIA.

5.5.1917: Torpedoed and sunk by German submarine UC 48 eight miles south east of Mine Head, Ireland in position 51.56 north by 07.24 west whilst on voyage from Montreal to London with general cargo. 45 lives were lost.

5. JELUNGA 1908

O.N. 98596 5,186g 3,371n 410.5 x 48.2 x 30.5 feet
Q. 4-cyl. by William Denny and Co., Dumbarton; 627 HP, 4,500 IHP, 15.8 knots (trial speed 16.3 knots)
80 first, 42 second, and 400 third class passengers.

30.10.1890: Launched by William Denny and Brothers, Dumbarton (Yard No. 442).

16.12.1890: Registered in the ownership of British India Associated Steamers Ltd., Glasgow as JELUNGA.

1893: Bareboat charter to Compañía Trasatlántica, Barcelona as a troopship. Registered in Spain as LEON X111.

1895: Returned to British India Associated Steamers Ltd., Glasgow and reverted to JELUNGA. Chartered again to Spain and renamed SANTIAGO.

6.1896: Returned to British India Associated Steamers Ltd., Glasgow and renamed JELUNGA.

7.1903: Owners became British India Steam Navigation Co. Ltd., London.

3.1908: Sold to Robertson, Shankland and Co. Ltd., London for the New York and Continental Line's Rotterdam-Halifax-New York emigrant service. Accommodation modified to 80 first and 1,000 third class passengers.

29.12.1908: Returned to British India Steam Navigation Co. Ltd., London.

7.1914: Sold to Bombay and Persia Steam Navigation Co. Ltd., Bombay and renamed JEHANGIR.

2.1917: Sold to Lau Siu Chien, Hong Kong

7.1919: Renamed WING SHING

7.1920: Sold by order of the Supreme Court, Hong Kong to Lau Wai Chun, Hong Kong.

1923: Sold to Man Chuen Steam Ship Co., Hong Kong.

18.8.1923: Wrecked during a typhoon at Hong Kong, later declared a constructive total loss and broken up in Hong Kong.

6. RAGLAN CASTLE 1909

O.N. 108187 4,324g 2,743n 383.5 x 46.3 x 20 feet
T. 3-cyl. by Barclay, Curle and Co. Ltd., Whiteinch; 419 HP, 2,600 IHP, 12.5 knots
36 first, 110 second, and 130 steerage passengers.
1909: 36 second and 550 steerage passengers.
20.1.1897: Launched by Barclay, Curle and Co. Ltd., Whiteinch (Yard No. 408).
3.1897: Completed.
8.1904: Returned to Barclay, Curle and Co. in part payment for new ships.
1905: Sold to the Russian Navy for use as a store-carrier.
2.1905: Sold to A/S Det Vestindiske Kompagni, Copenhagen for a West Indies service and renamed ST. DOMINGO
2 - 8.1906: Chartered for use as a troop ship between Vladivostock and Odessa.
23.9.1907: Arrived at Greenock following sale to Barclay, Curle and Co. Ltd., Glasgow.
1909: Renamed RAGLAN CASTLE.
3.1909: Chartered to North-West Transport Line for Rotterdam-Halifax-New York passenger service.
7.1909: Returned to Barclay, Curle and Co. Ltd., Glasgow.
1.1910: Sold to the Pythia Steam Ship Co. Ltd. (Donaldson Brothers, managers), Glasgow and renamed PYTHIA.
11.1911: Sold to A/S Dominion Whaling Co. Ltd. (T. Dannevig & Co.), Sandefjord and converted into a whale oil refinery.
1919: Manager became Chr. Christensen junior.
1920: Sold to A/S Odd (Chr. Christensen junior, managers), Sandefjord.
1923: Managers became I. Bryde and L. Thorsen.
1925: Manager became Thor Dahl.
18.4.1929: Capsized whilst being repaired at Sandefjord by Framnaes M.V. who took her over and repaired her.
1930: Sold to Hvalfanger A/S Africa (B. Gundersen, manager), Sandefjord and renamed READY.
1933: Manager became F. Bettum.
7.1934: Sold to Metal Industries Ltd., Rosyth.
12.9.1934: Arrived at Rosyth under tow.
10.1934: Demolition commenced.

7. NAPOLITAN PRINCE 1909-1910

O.N. 114432 2,900g 1,575n 363.5 x 42.2 x 25.3 feet
T. 3-cyl by Scott and Co., Greenock; 606 HP, 3,250 IHP, 14 knots.
75 first, 25 second, and 120 third class passengers.
1902: 25 first and 1,100 third class passengers.
1911: 16 first, 84 second, and 60 third class passengers.
1.7.1889: Launched by Scott and Co., Greenock (Yard No. 267).
8.1889: Completed for Mala Real Portuguesa, Lisbon as REI DE PORTUGAL.
10.1902: Sold to Prince Line Ltd. (J. Knott, manager), Newcastle-on-Tyne and renamed NAPOLITAN PRINCE. Placed on an Italy-New York emigrant service.
9.1909: Chartered to North-West Transport Line for a Rotterdam-Halifax-New York passenger service.
1.1910: Returned to Prince Line Ltd.
7.1911: Sold to Compagnie de Navigation Mixte, Marseilles and renamed MANOUBA.
2.1929: Sold to Italian shipbreakers.

8. SICILIAN PRINCE 1909-1910

O.N. 115845 2,784g 1,708n 363.5 x 42.2 x 25.3 feet
T. 3-cyl. by Scott and Co., Greenock; 606 HP, 3,250 IHP, 14 knots
75 first, 25 second, and 120 third class passengers.
1902: 25 first and 1,100 third class passengers.
28.9.1889: Launched by Scott and Co., Greenock (Yard No. 269).
11.1889: Completed for Mala Real Portuguesa, Lisbon as MOÇAMBIQUE.
1898: Renamed ALVARES CABRAL.
6.1902: Sold by Admiralty Court to William MacAndrew, London.
7.1902: Sold to Prince Line Ltd. (J. Knott, manager), Newcastle-on-Tyne and renamed SICILIAN PRINCE. Placed on Italy-New York emigrant service.

12.1909: Chartered to North-West Transport Line for Rotterdam-Halifax-New York passenger service.
4.1910: Returned to Prince Line Ltd.
1.1911: Sold to Khedivial Mail Steamship and Graving Dock Co. Ltd., London and renamed ABBASSIEH.
1930: Broken up in Italy

9. EKATERINA 1914-1915

O.N. 132662 1,209g 502n 245.1 x 34.5 x 14.6 feet
T. 3-cyl. by Ailsa Shipbuilding Co. Ltd., Troon; 193 HP, 1,980 IHP, 13 knots.
10.11.1911: Launched by the Ailsa Shipbuilding Co. Ltd., Troon (Yard No. 239).
27.2.1912: Registered in the ownership of the General Steam Navigation Co. Ltd., London as MAVIS.
16.9.1913: Sank following a collision in fog with the German steamer COLMAR (6,184/1912) near Maassluis in the New Waterway whilst on a voyage from London to Rotterdam with general cargo. One passenger was lost. Raised by Nieuwe Bergings Maatschappij, Maassluis.
20.2.1914: Register closed on sale to Dutch owners, but acquired by Canadian Northern Steamships Ltd., Toronto for use as an emigrant feeder ship between the Baltic and Rotterdam. Registered in the ownership of James Wishaw, Riga as EKATERINA.
8.1915: Requisitioned by the Russian Navy.
1918: Taken over by Government Baltic Steamship Co. and renamed FRANTS MERING. Some years later, transferred to the Government Black and Azov Seas Steamship Co., Odessa.
1960: Deleted from *Lloyd's Register*.

10. ROYAL GEORGE 1910-1922

O.N. 125643 10,897g 5,239n 525.8 x 60.2 x 27 feet
1910: 11,145g 5,685n
Steam turbines by the Fairfield Shipbuilding and Engineering Co. Ltd., Govan driving triple screws, 18,000 SHP, 14,500 IHP, 20.5 knots.
710 first, and 290 second class passengers.
1910: 344 first, 210 second, 560 third class passengers.
28.5.1907: Launched by the Fairfield Shipbuilding and Engineering Co. Ltd., Glasgow (Yard No. 449)
10.10.1907: Registered in the ownership of the Egyptian Mail Steam Ship Co. Ltd., London as HELIOPOLIS
2.1909: Egyptian Mail liquidated and ownership passed to the mortgagees, Fairfield Shipbuilding and Engineering Co. Ltd.
14.3.1910: Renamed ROYAL GEORGE.
26.4.1910: Sold to Canadian Northern Steamships Ltd., Toronto.
22.5.1916: Sold to Cunard Steam Ship Co. Ltd., Liverpool, but registered at London.
30.2.1919: Registered at Liverpool.
1920: Used as a floating hotel at Cherbourg. Later laid up in the River Fal.
25.7.1922: Register closed.
8.1922: Towed to Wilhelmshafen to be broken up.

11. ROYAL EDWARD 1910-1915

O.N. 125656 10,864g 5,659n 526.1 x 60.2 x 26.8 feet
1910: 11,117g 5,685n
Steam turbines by the Fairfield Shipbuilding and Engineering Co. Ltd., Govan driving triple screws; 18,000 SHP, 14,500 IHP, 20.5 knots
710 first, and 290 second class passengers.
1910: 344 first, 210 second, 560 third class passengers.
12.7.1907: Launched by the Fairfield Shipbuilding and Engineering Co. Ltd., Glasgow (Yard No. 450).
7.1.1908: Registered in the ownership of the Egyptian Mail Steam Ship Co. Ltd., London as CAIRO
2.1909: Egyptian Mail liquidated and ownership passed to the mortgagees, Fairfield Shipbuilding and Engineering Co. Ltd.
23.4.1910: Sold to Canadian Northern Steamships Ltd., Toronto.
29.4.1910: Renamed ROYAL EDWARD.
13.8.1915: Torpedoed by the German submarine UB 14 six miles west of Kandeliusa in position 36.31 north by 26.51 east whilst on a voyage from Avonmouth to Alexandria with 1,366 troops and a cargo of stores. 935 lives were lost.

PUTTING THE RECORD STRAIGHT

Letters, additions, amendments and photographs relating to articles in any issues of *Record* are welcomed. Letters may be lightly edited.

How to turn a potato ship turtle

The article about the unfortunate *John V* in *Record* 11 struck a number of chords in my memory. After many years superintending a fleet of small ships I came to dread an unexplained list or the presence of water where it shouldn't be. Experience taught me that the causes were invariably simple despite some surveyors who tried to complicate the issue or seafarers whose self-esteem refused to admit that human frailty could be a contributory factor. There were others, of course, who simply held up their hands in abdication and reported a mystery. In such cases, a mystery is quite the most unsatisfactory outcome to an investigation and regardless of any legal or commercial niceties, always left me profoundly disturbed.

Naturally there are a number of questions I would like to have asked and also a few items I should like to have inspected. That is now water well under the bridge and unfortunately the authors of the article could not find any evidence of an enquiry being held. Given that no lives were lost that is probably not too surprising. However, one imagines that the ship's underwriters would have wanted to know how and why the accident happened and it is probable that the owners and underwriters received a surveyor's report. But that was all a long time ago.

Clearly the ship had a stability problem that caused her to capsize. The nature of the problem is not so clear and was probably due to the combination of more than one factor. She was not apparently overloaded and the loaded weight of bagged potatoes was probably reasonably accurate. The 35 tons loaded on deck, probably spread evenly over the after hatch or in the well on the forward hatch, should not have caused her to capsize by itself. Not being able to calculate a stability condition it is impossible to say whether the ship had a negative GM and took up an angle of loll (the observed slight list to port) to regain marginally positive stability. Such a situation is relatively stable and some other factor must have acted on the ship to cause the accident.

If she was loaded to her marks on departure, no ballast water should have been taken after loading was complete although I do know that sometimes, once away from prying eyes, water will be put into one of the peak tanks to adjust the trim for one reason or another. This is usually pumped out again before entering the next port.

In my view, the additional factor was probably some slack water in the double bottom tanks. I note that she had lain in port for a couple of days before loading commenced. It is likely that the ballast water would have been pumped out more or less on arrival and, as is the unfortunate but normal practise, the engineer would knock off the pump as soon as it lost suction. Nobody would have sounded the tanks to check they were empty but, more seriously, it is highly probable that no further check was made. Entrained water would have drained towards the lowest point, a problem exacerbated if the tank valves were passing even a tiny amount of water. Unless the tanks were pumped again during the loading, there could easily have been sufficient slack water in the double bottom tanks to reduce the ship's stability due to the effect of free surface moments. This could have been made catastrophically worse if the centre keelson dividing the port and starboard tanks was not watertight. Noting that the ship was already thirteen years old and had survived the war when maintenance was probably minimal, there could easily have been some corrosion at the toe of the keelson.

It is obviously surmise but the description of how she had a small list that increased when she turned does suggest to me that there was sufficient free water in the tanks to cause the problem in conjunction with the small deck cargo.

The article brought back a number of painful memories, one in particular concerned an elderly ship loading soya meal on the inside berth at the Erith Oil and Cake Mills. Walking through the works, one could not see the ship until she came into view around the corner of a large shed. She was lying over at an improbable angle and my first reaction was to turn on my heel and disappear. The only reason that she had not gone right over was because her low side bilge was in the mud. There was slack water in all the tanks but of course it was a total mystery how it had got there because everybody was adamant that the tanks had been pumped dry! But that was the day before and nobody had checked then or subsequently.

I hope that all of this is of interest to your readers and helps to explain the accident. It will also be interesting to see if it stimulates any other similarly belated theories.

KEN GARRETT, 3 The Grange, East Mailing, Kent ME19 6AH

Blue flags, red faces

Just received *Record* 17 - probably the best ever! The colour section is a great addition, particularly as I used to see the Blue Star quartet so often in the Royals in London. I know I have commented before on the sheer quality of the photographs in *Record*, but the photo of *Politician* on page 2 really is magnificent. You mention elsewhere about those who prefer shots of ships at sea, but I really like views such as that of the *SAC Santander* at Livorno, which includes really atmospheric details such as the method of discharge of the grain and the local lighters, quite different from other types. I make ship models, and occasionally like to construct dioramas of ships in a setting such as a port working cargo - I think I will make one based on this photo!

The photo on page 11 is very interesting - can anyone identify the two-funneled ship alongside *PLM 7*? I have a feeling she is the Belgian cross-channel ship *Leopold II* built by Denny in 1892. She was sold to the British Shipping Administration in 1920 and broken up, probably in Germany, in 1923. Was she, in fact, broken up at Blyth?

Just a small correction - the Brocklebank houseflag was of course blue and white, not black and white as shown on page 45.

TONY SMYTHE, 35 Avondale Road, Rayleigh, Essex SS6 8NJ

We are pleased that colour is appreciated, but deeply embarrassed that Brocklebank's flag should have turned from blue to black in the processing of Louis Loughran's original artwork, in which the colour was a true blue, and we apologise to him. This resulted from a series of unforeseen circumstances, but was compounded by the editor responsible for this article being on holiday when colour proofs were checked. Thanks also to the many other readers who spotted this error. Brocklebank's flag is seen flying in the photograph of Mangla *on page 45.*

Snippets from 17

Page 9. *London Importer:* Her projected name was *Indiana*.

Page 10. PLM colliers: Congratulations on a very interesting article on so little known a topic - at least outside France. Was the full name of the railway Chemins de Fer de Paris et de Lyon à la Mediterranée, rather than as you had it? I have no immediate means of checking this, but my rather elementary knowledge of French would seem to indicate that this version makes better sense.

Page 16. *Blue Cross:* I don't think there is anything odd about the choice of colour in this ship's name. From 1890 to 1893 Rowland and Marwood went in for a series of crosses - *Red Cross* of 1890, *White Cross* of 1891, *Blue Cross* of 1892 and *Golden Cross* of 1893. The cross on the funnel no doubt started it off, but it was not confined to one, or even two, colours.

Page 26. *Leicestershire:* She and her sister, the *Warwickshire,* of 1948/49 were, unlike the pre-war Bibby ships, geared turbine steamers not motorships.

Page 63. *Huntsman* of 1904: I agree that it cannot possibly be a Boer War number, but it could easily be a First World War number. Troopships from Australia and New Zealand in 1914 were given numbers on the hull. Could the same system have been used on ships from India also?

BILL LAXON, Waimarana, Upper Whangateau Road, PO Box 171, Matakana 1240, New Zealand.

You have credited *New Zealand Star* on page 41 of *Record* 17 to me but it was actually a Bain Collection print.

I think the photograph of *Munkedal* on page 28 was one I took early on the misty morning of 5th March 1957 as she sped down Otago Harbour outward bound in ballast for the Persian Gulf. I was using a contact postcard camera at that time.

The Bank Line article in *Record* 17 brought back memories of the 1950s when all their Liberties were buzzing around in the Nauru phosphate trade. The later ships depicted in the article never had the 'character' or the 'characters' on board that used to prevail with the British-crewed Liberties. We used to have to get the police on many occasions to bring half the crew from the nearest pub to the ship and we were forever taking out warrants for deserters.
IAN FARQUHAR, PO Box 92, Dunedin, New Zealand

Every picture tells a story - *Record* 17
Although unable to identify the vessel pictured I am fairly certain of the location as I grew up in the area. It looks like the ferry hard in the High Street of the village of Rowhedge on the River Colne in Essex. Rowhedge is a short distance from the garrison town of Colchester and early in the First World War soldiers were billeted in the village. A bridge was built by the Royal Engineers to connect Rowhedge with the Wivenhoe marshes which was officially opened by King George V, but dismantled when the war ended.

The ferry that operated here was a flat-bottomed wooden craft that was either rowed or poled across depending on the state of the tide. As a teenager I crossed here daily to work in the shipyard of James W. Cook (Wivenhoe) Ltd. which was located on the opposite side slightly down river from Rowhedge.
R. SARGENT, 4 Ballajora Crossing, Maughold, Isle of Man IM7 1BA
Just before we received Mr. Sargent's letter, we heard from Bob Todd and David Hodge at the National Maritime Museum who had compared the photo with others in the NMM collection and arrived at the same conclusion about the port being Rowhedge. Now, if someone can just name the vessel...

The Stars of New Zealand
Having just read Captain Kinghorn's article in *Record* 17 I would like to add some relevant technical information regarding the last *Wellington Star* and *Southland Star*. They were the first fully automated ships under the British flag to be totally UMS (unmanned machinery space) for 16 hours a day (the first British ship with a UMS-style engine room was the *Clan Macgillivray* built in 1962). Although overall their accommodation and engine room were well appointed, they were not equipped with a permanent swimming pool nor was the engine control room air conditioned (a must for cooling sensitive electronics as well as engineers!) and both of the above were omitted with the typical Vestey retort that he did not want his officers going soft. As for the post-war *Wellington Star* class, accommodation was never Blue Star's strong point. I sailed on this class of vessel as a junior engineer in a cabin alongside no. 5 hatchway and shared a bulkhead with the crew bar and had a derrick post for company with winches on the deckhead, a practice continued on the SD 14.
A. D. FROST, 32 Oakfield Close, Sunderland, Tyne and Wear SR33RT

Goalposters recalled
Regarding the article 'The Furness Goalposters' in *Record* 17, in the 1930s I was a crew member of the *Manchester Regiment* for one year. This group of six ships were well built - they could maintain a speed of 14 knots even in fairly bad weather - but they were very expensive on fuel, burning at least 80 tons of coal each day, with 16 hungry furnaces. They had very hot stokeholds - they must have been almost unbearable in the Red Sea.

The *Manchester Regiment* was unique with her telescopic funnel. With one other of the group she also had a complete flying bridge, but which was never used for conning the ship. She also had a wireless telegraphy office and other cabins built right across the after boat deck. These appurtenances created a back eddy and caused smoke dispersal problems. The very last hold, number 7, was only used for

mooring ropes, so the three-ton derricks and Sampson posts were a waste of metal.

Their redeeming feature for 1922 cargo ships was that all crew were accommodated amidships. This was a double bonus as once a year they carried cattle pens on deck. With their lack of sheer and conical sterns they reminded me very much of the US 'Hog Island' ships.
N. WHITE, 67 Chart Downs, Dorking, Surrey RH5 4DF

Given that the Furness goalposters must have been ordered and designed before 1919, I wonder if strategic considerations played some part in their conception? With no sheer, flat sides, straight stems and cone-shaped sterns they required straightforward framing and plating, which simplified construction and must have saved time.

In 1942, the Furness Shipbuilding Company was asked to undertake the detailed development of the outline design for the standard fast general cargo liners, a design which had been worked out in the Sea Transport Department of the Ministry of War Transport. Perhaps Sir Amos Ayre had confidence in the residual experience and expertise in the Furness drawing office to get a fast cargo ship plan underway without undue delay. Certainly the finalisation of the general arrangement specifications, structural drawings, model resistance and other tests was achieved by May 1942. Implementation of the building programme was delayed because of more urgent wartime demands.
ALAN McCLELLAND, 33 Montclair Drive, Mossley Hill, Liverpool L18 0HB

'Sea Breezes' for March 1953 reported on page 209 that a number of £10 and 10s. notes, recognisable by their numbers, which went down when the Harrison liner *Politician* was wrecked in 1941 had made their appearance in Jamaica and Scotland Yard was reported to be co-operating with the Colonial authorities.

Before she ever put to sea as *London Merchant* she was damaged by being run into while completing on the Tees and before she was completed there were indications that the London to New York cargo service was falling off very rapidly with a surplus of tonnage so that, in the summer of 1923, she and her sister, the *London Shipper*, with others, were put on to a new service via the Panama Canal to the North Pacific, where her limited passenger accommodation proved tremendously popular and led to the specially-designed 'Pacific' class being built later.

At the end of 1924 she had an unpleasant experience at Portland, Oregon. Her store of liquor had been sealed by the Federal authorities but the local State Prohibition Director insisted on breaking the seals and seizing it. Naturally the British Embassy was annoyed by this breach of the agreement but not nearly as annoyed as the Federal authorities who were furious at being over-ridden by a local official, so that the liquor was returned to the ship and the offending official had to make full apology to the company. She was still on the Vancouver service when she was in collision on Christmas Eve 1927, but after that she was on the New York and Philadelphia run for a spell.

In April 1930 she was laid up at Tollesbury and remained there until she was sold to the Harrison Line in 1935 and renamed *Politician*. They employed her almost entirely on the East African run where she was very successful, but on 5th February 1941, she drove ashore in Eriskay Sound in the Outer Hebrides while on passage from Liverpool to the Gulf of Mexico with general cargo. She was refloated and beached but had to be abandoned as a total loss. 'Sea Breezes' reported that the appearance of some of the notes which were on board had caused a sensation.
FLOR VAN OTTERDYK, Antwerpsesteenweg 40, B-2070 Burcht, Belgium

Blue Star, Bank and Bibby
As might be expected, Captain Kinghorn has written a good account of those fine Blue Star cargo liners. I would, however, point out one minor error on page 40. The *New Zealand Star* of 1978 was a product of Smith's Dock, South Bank, and was not built at Haverton Hill.

A word of praise for Paul Boot's article and the finely

drawn illustrations of the types of vessel built at Sunderland for the Bank Line. The writer has gone to some length to point out the design variations which took place in post-war years and, although they are of interest, I was more inclined to note how little the Bank Line ships had changed over the years. If one follows the basic design from the pre-war *Eskbank*, the five-hatch arrangement with machinery amidships prevails through a period of some thirty years. Cargo gear and accommodation also remained much the same, although the ships themselves have increased in size - the length by about 20% and the beam by some 24%. Bank Line had obviously chosen a design of ship which suited their various trades over many years and they saw no reason to make any fundamental changes. Not many shipping lines could say that.

The caption under the photo of the *Derbyshire* on page 46 must be wrong. The *Derbyshire* was a conventional 'tween deck cargo ship, built by Bibbys for charter as a cargo liner. She and the *Worcestershire* marked Bibby's move into the charter market, once they appreciated that building ships essentially for the Burma trade had no future. I do not understand the reference to the *Derbyshire* having 'an unusually low freeboard', because the ship would have a conventional Load Line Certificate, for a 'tween decker, with steel hatch covers, issued by Lloyd's Register. Referring to the transfer to Bibby Bulk Carriers, I do not think that this had any significance either. In the 1970s Bibby Brothers created a number of shipping lines, within the group: Bibby Bulk Carriers Ltd. in 1972, Bibby Tankers Ltd. in 1973, Bibby Freighters Ltd. in 1974, Bibby Transport Ltd. in 1977. The fleet was distributed between these companies, but for reasons I do not know the ships were not necessarily listed under what might be said to be the appropriate heading. Thus Bibby Bulk Carriers fleet included dry-cargo ships, some oil/ore bulkers and a gas-carrier. I recall that in 1973 the Alexander cargo ship *Tenbury* briefly passed into Bibby's ownership, and the registered owners were Bibby Bulk Carriers Ltd. So the transfer of *Derbyshire* to Bibby Bulk Carriers did not mean that she was a bulker.

JOHN B. HILL, The Hollies, Wall, Hexham, Northumberland NE46 4EQ

Paul Boot responds: When I blithely referred to Derbyshire *as a bulk carrier, what I should have said was that she was designed particularly for the carriage of bulk cargoes. As John Hill has rightly pointed out, she did have a second cargo deck and must therefore be classed as a general cargo ship. In search of evidence of her bulk handling capabilities, I carried out a cursory survey of the tonnage figures on a random selection of shelter deck cargo ships of similar approximate size, built during the 1960s, and compared these with bulk carriers of similar vintage. The ratio of deadweight to net tonnages gives some indication of the role for which the ship*

has been designed; with a higher figure favouring heavy, densely stowed (i.e. bulk) cargoes, and a lower figure favouring general cargoes with a lesser stowage factor, where volume is more important. The average of nine typical shelter deck vessels comes out at 2.455, with the highest, Radcliffe's Llanwern *of 1962, at 2.58. The average of four geared bulk carriers (it was difficult to readily find any more in this tonnage range) is 2.688. The figure for* Derbyshire *is 2.64, the same as Trader Navigation's* Scottish Trader. *I leave the demolition of my argument to those more versed in naval architectural matters.*

Engineering matters

On opening *Record* 16, I found there were two subjects on which I have a contribution to make.

My brother Harry G. Wood was Third Officer on the steamer *St. Margaret* on her maiden voyage in 1936. He tells me that the ship sailed from Cardiff for Brazilian ports and Buenos Aires, carrying 12 passengers and general cargo. However, the ship had to put into the Cape Verde Islands due to problems with the White engine. There they stayed until the next company ship arrived with spares more than two weeks later. Harry made several voyages in the ship, but does not recall any further problems.

In 1950 I served as Second Engineer on Strick Line's steamer *Albistan*. Strick ships were usually built by Readheads at South Shields and fitted with triple-expansion engines with Bauer Wach exhaust turbines. However, *Albistan* (5,516/1948) had been purchased on the stocks at Short Brothers Ltd., Sunderland and was equipped with a reheat engine.

With the reheat engine, a fuel economy of 15% was claimed through reheating the steam between the intermediate and high pressure cylinders, aided no doubt by the simplified flow through the poppet valves. I recall that, voyage after voyage, *Albistan* was consuming under 0.9 pounds of fuel oil/IHP/hour at 12 knots.

Regarding the White engine, a fuel economy of 40% could have been achieved through double reheat and up to 20% more with the exhaust turbine (see 'Steam at Sea' by D. Griffiths, Conway Press) so that the claim of 40% economy sounds believable.

I doubt whether a double compound engine at 500 rpm would have been more significantly more thermally efficient, although mechanical efficiency may well have been higher.

PHILIP E. WOOD, Brockwells Cottage, Caerwent, Caldicott, Monmouthshire NP26 5AJ

Albistan had an engine by George Clark (1938) Ltd., who were presumably building reheat engines under licence from North Eastern Marine Engineering Co. Ltd. The two companies later merged. Ed.

Bill Laxon has kindly supplied this photograph of *Ventnor* (3,961/1901) of Gow, Harrison and Co. leaving Westport, New Zealand on her last voyage, as described in Ian Muir's article 'Soot, Seawater, and Cylinder Oil' in *Record* 16. On 27th October 1902, the *Ventnor* struck a reef off Cape Egmont and sank, eight lives being lost as her officers and crew struggled to get ashore in the ship's boats.

A COUNTRY SHIP
John Naylon

As if emerging from the previous century, the barque *Nithyakalyani* leaves Akyab, Burma, with rice for her home port of Jaffna, Ceylon, in 1938. She flies the Red Ensign. The picture was taken by the late Captain George V. Clark of Whitley Bay, who photographed many such vessels in the 1930s, and is kindly provided by Captain A.W. Kinghorn.

The rice trade across the Bay of Bengal was one of those niches of maritime activity (along with Australian grain, Baltic timber and West Indies logwood) in which square sail was still able to earn a modest living in the interwar years. Throughout the 'twenties and 'thirties a fleet of wooden brigs, brigantines, barques and barquentines, ranging from 200 to 700 tons burden, operated along the coasts of Malabar, Coromandel, the Maldives, the Laccadives, the Gulf of Mannar, Ceylon, Burma and sometimes even Malaya and Siam. Many had been built during and soon after the First World War, but some were still being launched as late as 1937 (for instance, the barquentine *Parathavarthaniamma*).

These 'country ships' maintained the appearance and traditions of the European sailing vessels of the mid-nineteenth century in their hull forms and rigs. The terms 'country ships' or 'country craft' were held to include vessels owned by Englishmen resident in India as well as ships Indian-built, owned and managed, and seem to have been used as far back as the seventeenth century. Some Indians regarded the terminology as pejorative - especially if expressed as 'country wallahs' - but it was widely used by the Indian Government itself (as in Country Craft Insurance, the Country Craft Organization Office and the Country Craft Advisory Committee) and in the private sector (for example, the Country Craft Trades Association, a forum for owners, shippers, brokers and captains).

Built in Jaffna, Tuticorin or Rangoon, country ships were almost all constructed of Malabar or Burmese teak, sometimes even to the masts and spars, although teak was not really apt for this purpose, being too stiff and inflexible. Thingyan pine was a more suitable material for the top hamper. Accordingly, country ships were long-lived: up to 65 years or more. K.B. Vaidya estimated the building costs of a Jaffna barque as around 40,000 rupees in 1945. Design was a matter of tradition and rule of thumb, without the use of plans or models, but the hull lines were generally pleasing, with relatively fine ends, and the vessels could achieve 7 to 10 knots. They drew rather little water - only 10 to 12 feet loaded. The hull profile was without sheer amidships (slightly hogged in the case of the *Nithyakalyani*) but with a characteristically up-tilted bow and stern. The upswept line of the wale forward, continued along the top of the stem head above the billethead, gave the impression of an upturned snout, very pronounced in our picture. This projecting bow may have evolved from the beakhead of the galley via the Indian coasting *grab*. The stern usually ended in a square transom, although some vessels had elliptical counters and there were even some double-enders. Only the biggest vessels boasted a raised poop like the *Nithyakalyani*.

To the very end the country ships carried the rig of the mid-nineteenth century. Huge single topsails, which began to be superceded in Britain in the 1850s and 1860s, were the rule, with the *Nithyakalyani* proving the exception (off the *Nithyakalyani*'s starboard quarter there appears to be a brigantine with an enormous fore course and single topsail). The sail plan of the larger vessels was often lofty, including fancy kites such as skysails and stunsails in the style of the old clippers. The *Nithyakalyani*, for instance, sports fore and main skysails, four headsails and three main and mizzen staysails. A curiosity is the small portable jigger mast and sail mounted on the taffrail, the purpose of which was to make her handier in stays. Other photographs of the barque show her without this device.

Masts were stepped vertically, without rake, or even stayed forward. Standing rigging was of heavy coir except for the lanyards, which were of hemp. The shrouds were rarely provided with ratlines, saying much for the agility of the crews; at most there might be a few battens across the lower shrouds, which were set up to outside channels with deadeyes and lanyards. Long jibbooms extended beyond the bowsprit. Sails were of heavy local cotton.

The masters (*tindels*) of the country ships were invariably Hindus, as were most of the crews, who would number 15 to 25 according to the size of the ship and who were seasonally employed - say for 8 or 9 months of the year. Family connections were strong amongst the crews, who would attach themselves to a particular master. Captains and crews were paid on a share of the ship's earnings, as in whaling. The *tindel* was responsible for paying the crew and also acted autonomously as to the sale and purchase of cargoes, loading and unloading (done by the crew), provisioning, repairs and the handling of business.

There was no crew accommodation on board, as such - just a clear space under the poop deck, for the full width of the ship, without bulkheads or partitions, serving as store room, sail locker, bosun's locker and living quarters for the master and helmsmen. Here too all hands might congregate in bad weather; otherwise the rest of the crew slept under the shallow three-foot high open forecastle head.

A feature which always excited western comment was the country ships' extraordinarily long names, usually composite words with a religious or devotional connotation, invoking gods and goddesses in the Hindu pantheon in order to ensure protection, guidance and a prosperous voyage. Some which have been recorded are those of the brigs *Athiyathurraman (The Great God Rama), Bhyalkshmy (Lkshmy, Holy Goddess of Wealth)* and *Dhanaletchmy (Dhana, Goddess of Wealth)*, the barquentine *Parathavarthaniamma (Mother of the Water*

World), and the barques *Nithyakalyani (Nithyakalyani, The Beautiful Wife of Lord Siva), Sivasupramaniapuravny (The Wife of Lord Siva)* and *Venyagasowpakialetchmy (The God Ganash and the Healthy and Wealthy Goddess Lechmy)*.

Freights were high enough, and labour cheap and plentiful enough, to enable the country ships to earn a living from two or three voyages a year. They carried coconuts, coconut oil, copra, coir and coir matting from Ceylon to Malabar, Tuticorin, Madras, Burma and Siam, and food grains, piece goods and other general cargo from India; but the big annual cargo was rice from Rangoon and Akyab to Colombo, Jaffna and Indian ports, a distance of some 1,300 nautical miles. During the south-west monsoon the square-riggers were usually laid up in Colombo or Jaffna, along with the locally-owned coasting dhows. The sailing season started with the change of the monsoon at the end of September. The passage north-east from Ceylon in sand ballast took three or four weeks; upper yards and even topgallant masts were commonly sent down, and passages made under courses and topsails only. The masters navigated by sailing down the latitude. They carried a compass and shot their noon latitude, but very few vessels had a chronometer and longitude was determined by dead reckoning. Prior to the Second World War, virtually no ships or cargoes were insured (or insurable).

Some remnants of this anachronistic fleet lasted into the early 1950s. Brigs were said to be still common at Colombo and Cochin in the 1940s. In the 1950s the Sultan of the Maldives owned the 200-ton brig *Athiyathurraman*, which made three voyages a year between Ceylon and the islands and also served as his yacht; he also owned a small brigantine which according to Basil Greenhill was still afloat in 1952. K.S. Vaidya states that in 1945 some 5,300 sailing vessels, mostly of the dhow type, were operating on the west coast of India. There had been considerable building during the Second World War, especially from 1941 onwards, and this continued vigorously in the immediate postwar years.

SOURCES AND ACKNOWLEDGEMENTS

Photographs are from the collection of John Clarkson unless otherwise credited. We thank all who gave permission for their photographs to be used, and for help in finding photographs we are particularly grateful to Tony Smith, Jim McFaul and David Whiteside of the World Ship Photo Library; to Ian Farquhar, Bill Laxon, Peter Newall, Ivor Rooke, William Schell, George Scott; to David Hodge and Bob Todd of the National Maritime Museum; and other museums and institutions listed.

Themes and variations: the development of the post-war Bank Line cargo ships
The genesis for this article was some brief notes and sketches produced by Graham Thursby many years ago as an aid to identification of the Doxford series.
Bank Line 1885-1985 Appleyard HS, World Ship Society, Kendal, 1985
British Tramps and their Peacetime Contribution to World Shipping History. Stewart IG, Ian Stewart Marine Publications, 1997
Liberty Ships in Peacetime Stewart IG, Ian Stewart Marine Publications, 1992.
The Doxford Economy Ship, Frost AD, *Ships Monthly*, February 1989.
Bank Line (commerative booklet) The Journal of Commerce, Liverpool, 1955.
The Motor Ship, 1947-1973.
Shipping and Transport, 1962-1965.
Particular thanks are due to former Bank Line Superintendent Engineer, Mr. R. MacLeod; Captains R. A. Leach and F. B. Rodgers, for providing a wealth of information on the construction and operation of these vessels; to Ian Rae for the information on the Swan, Hunter built ships, and to Captains K. S. Garrett, D. Glass, and W. Langworthy, and Alan McClelland for their various contributions.

Herring and caviar to Canada
This feature came about after a conversation with Martin Lindenborn who owns a wonderful collection of glass negatives taken in the early 1900s by Cornelis Nieuwland of Rotterdam. Martin kindly provided

most of the photos and some useful information. Thanks also to David Burrell for helping to unravel the complex world of William Petersen, Kevin Griffin for much Canadian information, John Lingwood for help with turret ships, Maurizio Eliseo and Luis Miguel Correeia; and as always to Roy Fenton, Bill Laxon and Bill Schell for checking the fleet list. As well as Noel Bonsor's notes for *North Atlantic Seaway*, now part of the World Ship Society's collection, the following sources were consulted:
The Royal Route to Canada by R.M. Parsons: *Ships Monthly* October and November 1984
Seagoing experience of Captain F.J. Thompson Sea Breezes September and October 1960
The Doxford Turret Ships Gray L & Lingwood J, World Ship Society, Kendal, 1975
Idyll of the Kings Mallett A World Ship Society, Kendal, 1980
Those Elegant Edwardian Liners by Peter Kohler, *Ship Aficionado*
Steam Operations on the lower St. Lawrence to 1914 by Kenneth Mackenzie, Seaports and the Shipping World November 1985 and August 1991
Various articles from *The Scanner*, bulletin of the Toronto Marine Historical Society

A country ship
There is discussion and photographs of country craft, using notes supplied by Captain G.V. Clark, in *Deep-Water Sail* Underhill HA, Brown, Son & Ferguson, Glasgow, 1952, pp.75-8 and also in 'Some Indian and Country Craft' by R.H. Turner, in Alex. A. Hurst, *The Medley of Mast and Sail*, Volume II, Teredo Books, Brighton, 1981, pp.121-37. For an historical background to the country trade see, *The Old 'Country Trade' of the East Indies*, Coates WH, Imray, Laurie, Norie and Wilson, Ltd., London, 1911, reprinted by Cornmarket Press, London, 1969. K.B. Vaidya supplies very detailed information of almost every aspect of the trade in *The Sailing Vessel Traffic on the West Coast of India and its Future*, The Popular Book Depot, Bombay, 1945. Translations from the Tamil are kindly provided by Nirmala Rajendran.

THE FRED. OLSEN CRUISE SHIPS
Anthony Cooke

Norwegian but very anglophile, the Olsen family of Oslo have over the years owned an enormous variety of vessels, ranging from sailing ships to cargo liners and tankers and from drilling rigs to ferries and cruise ships. They have had a long connection with the Canary Islands and still run ferry services there. They have also had considerable industrial interests and hold a large stake in the Harland and Wolff shipyard at Belfast.

Fredrik Olsen (1857-1933) went into shipowning in 1886. He was actually the second family member to bear that name. His father, the first Fredrik, owned a number of sailing ships. The young Fred., too, started with sailing vessels but in 1897 took delivery of his first steamship, the *Bayard*. Most Olsen ships since then have been given names beginning with the letter B. In 1899, Olsen moved his business from the family's home village of Hvitsten to nearby Christiania, the present day Oslo. Many years later, in a sentimental gesture, his grandson, also Fred. Olsen, registered his best-known ship, the second *Black Prince*, at Hvitsten for a time.

By the early years of the twentieth century, the second Fred. Olsen had become one of the most prominent of the thrusting Norwegians who made their country – not yet independent and with a tiny population – the fourth biggest shipowning nation in the world. By a series of acquisitions of other businesses, he entered the liner trades between Norway and the Continent and Britain and, very significantly, the fruit trades from the Mediterranean and the Canary Islands to northern Europe. By the 1930s, the Olsens owned a fine fleet of motor fruit-carriers. Olsen ships became famous for the beautiful bronze figureheads which decorated their new-style rounded bows, which had superseded the old straight stems. I have heard it said that some of these figureheads still exist on the family's Scottish estate.

It was particularly on the routes between Norway and Britain that Fred. Olsen became involved in the passenger trade, especially after his purchase in 1906 of Det Ostland Lloyd, which ran a mail, passenger and cargo service between southern Norwegian ports and the Tyne. For many years, Olsens maintained this route with steamers of less than 2,000 gross tons, but in 1938 they moved into a new league with the introduction of the first *Black Prince* and *Black Watch*. These were immensely stylish 5,000-ton motorships built at Oslo by the Olsen-owned Akers shipyard. Alas, both were sunk during the war and although *Black Prince* was salvaged, hopes of rebuilding her were eventually abandoned.

Post-war rebuilding

It was not until 1951 and 1953 that worthy replacements could be completed. They were, of course, small liners rather than cruise ships but nevertheless they merit attention in this article. Named *Blenheim* and *Braemar*, they had a strangely mixed parentage. They had been ordered from the Akers yard but the construction of their hulls was sub-contracted to John I. Thornycroft and Co. Ltd. at their Woolston yard in Southampton. They were towed to Oslo, where Akers themselves installed the engines and dealt with the fitting-out. Of 4,700 tons gross, the two ships were notable examples of 1950s streamlining, particularly in respect of their unusual aerodynamic funnels which, it was claimed, projected smoke and soot well clear of the ship in all weathers. There was space for about 40 cars, which were lifted on and off by crane, as was then customary. The name *Blenheim* was chosen as a tribute to the great British wartime leader Winston Churchill, who had been an inspiration for many Norwegians during the Nazi occupation of their country. A large photograph of him was hung in one of the ship's lounges. (Blenheim Palace is the family seat of the Churchill family. A more direct tribute came from Denmark when, shortly after his death, DFDS chose the name *Winston Churchill* for their latest ferry.) The *Blenheim* was seriously damaged by fire in 1968 and never returned to the company's service, but the *Braemar* persisted until 1975, by which time she was the last of the 'classic' North Sea passenger vessels.

A joint project

The next generation of Fred. Olsen passenger ships came about, it is said, because of an informal meeting between the third Fred. Olsen and the managing director of the Bergen Line at which they discussed the problems they were facing. There was an increasing demand from passengers wishing to take their cars with them when they crossed the North Sea. Olsens also needed new and larger tonnage to cope with the wintertime fruit traffic from the Canary Islands to Britain. The result was a joint order by the two companies for a most unusual 9,500-ton ship

Continued on page 104

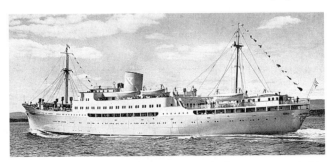

Two views of the *Black Prince* whose design was remarkably 'modern' for 1938. [Both: Peter Newall collection]

Also well ahead of their time in external styling were the *Blenheim* of 1951 (above) and the *Braemar* of 1953, the latter photographed at North Shields (below). *[Upper: Laurence Dunn collection, lower: Malcolm Donnelly]*

FROM TANKER TO FERRY Part 2
Frank Heine and Roland Whaite

Although the *Heleanna* disaster had discouraged shipowners from pursuing any further passenger conversions, the *Efthycosta II* had shown the viability of a freight to ro-ro transformation. At about the same time, Norwegian shipowner Leif Hoegh had taken two former Esso tankers, the *Genova* and the *Winchester*, and sent them to Rijeka for transformation into the car carriers *Hoegh Trader* (21,364/1958) and *Hoegh Transporter* (21,670/1958), whilst Seatrain Lines of the USA had already converted a number of T2 tankers to carry road and rail vehicles, albeit that the loading was mostly done using cranes.

Traghetti del Mediterraneo s.p.a.
This title literally translates as 'The Mediterranean (shareholding) Ferry Company' and refers to an operation initially providing freight ferry services from Genoa to a range of ports in Sardinia and Sicily. Established in 1965, and bringing a series of vessels carrying *Espresso* names into service from 1967, by 1971 the fleet consisted of nine ro-ros, the smallest coming in at just under 2,000 tons gross, and including services also from Livorno.

In 1972, the sale of the newest member of the fleet, *Espresso Veneto* (4,567/1971), to a Libyan company coincided with the desire to expand operations outside the Tyrrhenian Sea, and Traghetti del Mediterraneo purchased the tanker *Marilen* from COSATMAR of Cagliari; she was then moved to the San Marco yard in Trieste, across the northern end of the Adriatic from where she had been built in Venice for Palermo owners eighteen years previously.

The removal of the oil tanks, pipelines, pumping mechanisms and tank exhausts was followed by the installation of the main trailer deck within the hull. Unlike the Greek conversions, which all made use of side doors, the main access was created through a bulky, hinged bow visor. Two parallel ramps at the break of the forecastle enabled trailers to reach the weather deck.

Even more dramatically, the entire amidships superstructure block was shifted aft to be merged with the existing afterhouse, some space also being created within that block to extend the vehicle lanes.

The career of the *Espresso Marilen*
Although having a bigger hull (557 x 72 x 30 feet) all round than the *Efthycosta II* (515 x 64 x 30 feet), the gross tonnage of the now *Espresso Marilen* was set at 8,398 when delivered nearly a year later to her new owners. Registered in Porto Torres on the island of Sardinia, *Espresso Marilen* re-entered service on 13th October 1973 and was soon trading not only from Italy to the Red Sea and Persian Gulf, but also to West Africa and within the Mediterranean to Libya.

These remained her principal routes even when out on charter, and it was on one such voyage from Cagliari to Lagos that she was in collision with the Algerian ro-ro *Collo* (1,598/1973) 60 miles off the Spanish coast on 4th October 1978. Only four crew members, out of a total of 30, survived the sinking of the *Collo* which was heading from Algeria towards Marseilles, and the bow damage to the *Espresso Marilen* required a period of repair in Genoa.

The *Espresso Marilen* was back on the West Africa service during 1979, but went into lay-up at Genoa during November because of increasing financial difficulties for the Gruppo Magliveras, responsible for both Traghetti del Mediterraneo and the ferries of Trans-Tirreno Express. She was then acquired by the long-established company of Ignazio Messina, and was towed to La Spezia in March 1981.

During the ensuing months, the superstructure and most of the machinery was removed, and a three-storey framework constructed on the hull to accommodate cars. For five years, the former *Espresso Marilen* served as 'Terminal Messina', a floating garage for temporary holding of cars for export out of La Spezia but, in 1986, Ignazio Messina dispensed with this add-on framework whilst still occasionally finding it useful to use the old hull as a stand for containers.

In 1996, Messina moved his home port to Genoa, and it was from there that the remains of the *Espresso Marilen* were towed to Turkey for dismantling in July 1997.

Stages in the career of
Espresso Marilen.
Opposite: as the tanker
Marilen [*Fotoflite
incorporating Skyfotos*]
Top and middle: as
converted in 1972-1973:
note the bow doors in the
top photo. [*Both: Antonio
Scrimali*]
Bottom: laid up at La
Spezia before conversion
to a floating garage. The
bow visor is in the raised
position. [*Battaglia
Salvatore, World Ship
Photo Library collection*]

A trio for Dolphin Shipping

The final company to embark on a conversion programme was another Greek operation, the apparently short-lived Dolphin Shipping Company. They first acquired the tanker *Damianos* and gave it back its original name of *Tabriz* as bestowed by Wilh. Wilhelmsen in 1954. Built by Eriksbergs in Gothenburg, she had served Wilhelmsen for 13 years before her first sale, and her second spell as *Tabriz* lasted for another year in the tanker trades.

During 1976 she was renamed *Dolphin Elena* and moved to the Mariotti yard in Genoa. Her transformation to a ro-ro freight ferry produced yet another variation on the theme, vehicle access being arranged through two large stern doors incorporating shoreside ramps; these doors were at the after end of a pair of box-like structures, either side of the engine room, which also contained the internal ramps. A total lane length of over 5,500 feet was created by raising the midships superstructure, as in the *Efthycosta II*. Registered in Limassol and under the management of Spiro Magliveras - indicating a strong connection with Traghetti del Mediterraneo - *Dolphin Elena* entered service in 1977 from Italy to West Africa re-measured at less than half her original gross tonnage.

Two more tankers were acquired during 1976, originally the sisters *Saint Remi* and *Saint Thierry* of Compagnie Francaise d'Armament of Bordeaux, and both locally built by Forge et Chantiers de la Gironde. The former had become firstly the *Marignan* and then the Liberian *Iliade*, whilst *Saint Thierry* had experienced only the one previous change, to *Olympie* (including a period of lay-up on the River Fal), before being taken over as *Dolphin Lucia* and *Dolphin Patricia*.

Initially, both vessels were laid up near Piraeus, but *Dolphin Lucia* left for Palermo on 16th December 1976, whilst *Dolphin Patricia* followed on 25th February 1977. The bridge of each vessel was moved aft, with a passageway for vehicles on the port side of the accommodation. A pair of stern quarter ramps combined with internal ramps to give access to both the enclosed and upper trailer decks. Total lane length was little different from that of *Dolphin Elena*.

With the two latest vessels joining *Dolphin Elena* at the end of 1977 and in the spring of 1978, services were not only concentrated from the Mediterranean to West Africa and the Red Sea, but extended into Northern waters and especially to Hamburg and Rostock. Dolphin acquired another vessel during this period, the tanker *Braconda* (12,805/1960), but there is no suggestion that there was any intention to convert *Dolphin Olivia* and she was only kept for one year.

Final activities

In 1979, ownership of all three vessels changed to one-ship

During conversion of *Tabriz* (seen above, in Wilhelmsen colours) to *Dolphin Elena* (below) two large stern ramps were fitted, well displayed in the lowest photograph. *[Top: World Ship Photo Library Brownell collection, others: Antonio Scrimali]*

companies and, whilst the *Dolphin* element was dropped from each name, registration stayed in Cyprus, and the routes were relatively unchanged.

On 29th September 1980, fire broke out on *Elena* about 100 nautical miles south east of Safaga in the Red Sea. After a night of unsuccessful fire fighting, the crew left the ship, but she was subsequently towed in to Aqaba and the fire extinguished. The damaged vessel arrived under tow at Piraeus on Christmas Day 1980, carrying the name *Adventure I* and was rebuilt during the following year at Perama.

Placed on the Greek registry, and in the hands of a John S. Latsis subsidiary, *Adventure I* saw service between the Mediterranean, the Red Sea and the North Sea for two years until again being laid up near Salamis in November 1983.

Another stern ramp conversion, *Dolphin Lucia* is seen about to enter the Kiel Canal (above). *[Michael Cassar]*

On conversion, *Saint Thierry* (above) was renamed *Dolphin Patricia* which became simply *Patricia* in 1979 (below). *[Above: Fotoflite incorporating Skyfotos; below: Antonio Scrimali]*

After joining many other Latsis vessels in Eleusis Bay, the *Adventure I* had one final flurry of activity when she was sold in August 1988 to become *Speedo*, working for about a month until returning to Piraeus on 15th October. A further change to *Champion* only slightly delayed her last voyage to Indian breakers, arriving at the beginning of April 1989 in Mangalore.

Lucia and *Patricia* continued to have somewhat parallel careers, becoming in 1981 respectively the *Welcome* and the *Welfare III*. Both ships were registered under the Panamanian flag, and were managed by Unifida S.A, the shipping arm of the Overseas Trust Bank based in Lugano, Switzerland.

Operating areas stayed much as before, and charters were obtained from Polish Ocean Lines and later from Deutsche Seereederei in Rostock. Both vessels were to transit the Kiel Canal often, delivering East German IFA trucks to West Africa and the Middle East.

In 1982, *Welfare III* was provided with an additional deck extending from the break of the forecastle to just forward of the bridge, increasing the available lane length to around 8,000 feet. Still chartered to DSR, her voyaging took her as far afield as China, delivering her last load to Xingang in mid-November 1986 before proceeding to Kaohsiung for scrapping.

In the meantime, *Welcome* had also ventured further afield under charter to Brazilian company Transroll and was on one of its regular transits between Italy and Brazil when she suffered an engine room explosion off the Liberian coast, sinking on 29th January 1986, fortunately without any loss of life.

Thus, the three former Dolphin vessels all had useful careers and ranged much more widely than the Efthymiadis predecessors in demonstrating the commercial viability of this change of use for redundant tankers.

Welcome in the Kiel Canal (upper) and *Welfare III* with an additional deck fitted (lower).
[Upper: Michael Cassar; lower: Antonio Scrimali]

Conversions in Italian yards

8. ESPRESSO MARILEN 1972-1981

Italian O.N. 50 (LR: 5224522) 8,398g 4,060n 169.78 x 22.05 x 9.23 metres

9-cyl. 2SCSA oil engine by S.A. Fiat S.G.M., Turin; 7,000 BHP, 14 knots.

23.1.1954: Launched by Cantieri Navale Breda, Venice (Yard No. 156) for Sicula Azionari Trasporti Marittimi S.p.a, Palermo as MARILEN.

10.1954: Completed (12,631g 7,245n 18,179dwt).

1971: Sold to Compagnia Sarda Trasporti Marittima S.p.a. (COSATMAR), Cagliari.

1972: Sold to Traghetti del Mediterraneo S.p.a. (Spiro P. Magliveras), Genoa.

25.10. 1972: Arrived at Arsenali Triestino San Marco S.A.,Trieste for conversion to ro-ro.

1973: Renamed ESPRESSO MARILEN and registered at Porto Torres.

4.10.1978: In collision with the Algerian motor vessel COLLO (1,598/1873) 60 miles east of Cabo de Palos, Cartagena in position 37.45 north by 00.16 east. COLLO sank with the loss of 26 out of her crew of 30.

1978-1979: Under repair in Genoa.

11.1979: Laid up in Genoa.

3.1981: Sold to Ignazio Messina, Genoa.

1981-1986: Served as 'Terminal Messina', a floating garage at La Spezia.

1986-1996: Hulk remained in La Spezia.

1996: Hulk towed to Genoa.

11.7.1997: Arrived at Aliaga for demolition by Sök Ltd.

Top: *Marilen* in the New Waterway on 30th August 1969. *[World Ship Photo Library]*
Above: As *Espresso Marilen.* *[Frank Heine collection]*
Below: As 'Terminal Messina' on 16th July 1997 soon after arrival at Aliaga for demolition. *[Selim San]*

Adventure I transiting the Suez Canal in 1983. *[James L. Shaw, World Ship Photo Library collection]*

9. DOLPHIN ELENA/ELENA/ADVENTURE I/SPEEDO/CHAMPION 1976-1989

Cyprus O.N. 374213 (LR: 5348299) 5,383g 3,277n
170.52 x 21.34 x 6.03 metres.
Burmeister & Wain 8-cyl. 2SCSA oil engine by Eriksbergs M/V A/B, Gothenburg; 10,000 BHP, 16.25 knots.
4.3.1954: Launched by Eriksbergs M/V A/B, Gothenburg (Yard No. 480) for Wilhelm Wilhelmsen, Oslo as TABRIZ
12.5.1954: Completed (11,747g 6,824n 18,010dwt).
8.1967: Sold to Astro Vencedor Compania Naviera S.A., Panama (Shipping and Transport Agencies Ltd. (A.G. Papadakis, E.P. Spiliotapoulos and C.M. Gliptis), Piraeus, managers), registered in Monrovia and re-named DAMIANOS.
1975: Sold to Dolphin Shipping Co. Ltd., Limassol (Traghetti del Mediterraneo S.p.a. (Spiro P. Magliveras), Genoa, managers) and renamed TABRIZ.
1976: Arrived at the Temistocle Mariotti yard, Genoa for conversion to a ro-ro and renamed DOLPHIN ELENA.
1979: Sold to Ciel Shipping Ltd., Piraeus, renamed ELENA and registered in Limassol.
29.9.1980: Fire broke out south east of Safaga in Red Sea.
30.9.1980: Crew abandoned vessel in position 26.27 north by 35.17 east.
10.1980: Towed to Aqaba and fire extinguished.
12.1980: Acquired by Aegis Compania Naviera S.A., Panama (John S. Latsis, Athens, manager).
25.12.1980: Arrived in tow at Piraeus for rebuilding under the name ADVENTURE I and registered in Piraeus.
12.11.1983: Laid up near Salamis; managers reported as Bilinder Marine Corp S.A.
8.1988: Sold to Corpus S.A., Monrovia (Intertrans Shipping Ltd. (Stylianos Markakis), Piraeus, managers), registered in Kingstown, St Vincent and renamed SPEEDO.
10.1988: Re-named CHAMPION and laid up near Salamis.
1.4.1989: Arrived at Mangalore for demolition by Nathani Industrial Services.
15.5.1989: Demolition commenced.

10. DOLPHIN LUCIA/LUCIA/WELCOME 1976-1986

Cyprus O.N. 380878 (LR No.: 5306708) 6,354g 2,949n
175.34 x 22.51 x 10.38 metres
Burmeister & Wain 7-cyl. 2SCSA oil engine by Société Forges et Ateliers du Creusot, Le Creusot; 8,750 BHP, 16.25 knots.
29.11.1958: Launched by Forges et Chantiers de la Gironde, Bordeaux (Yard No. 239) for Compagnie Francaise d'Armament Maritime, Bordeaux as SAINT REMI.
1959: Completed (13,631g 8,185n 20,650dwt).
1966: Sold to Courtage et Transports S.A., Paris and renamed MARIGNAN
1968: Sold to Transoceanic Transportation Co., Monrovia (Courtage et Transports S.A., Paris, managers) and

renamed ILIADE.
1974: Owners became Stardust Shipping Co. S.A., Monrovia (Courtage et Transports S.A., Paris, managers).
1975: Managers became Transoceanic Transportation Co., Piraeus.
1976: Sold to Dolphin Shipping Co. Ltd., Limassol (Traghetti del Mediterraneo S.p.a. (Spiro P. Magliveras), Genoa, managers) and renamed DOLPHIN LUCIA.
18.12.1976: Arrived at Bacini Siciliana S.p.a., Palermo for conversion to ro-ro.
1979: Sold to Arsera Marine Co. Ltd., Limassol (Mediterranean and Overseas Shipping Agencies S.p.a. (Fotis G. Poulides), Genoa, managers) and renamed LUCIA.
1981: Sold to Transafric Co. Inc., Monrovia (Unifida S.A., Lugano, managers), renamed WELCOME and registered in Panama.
29.1.1986: Abandoned and sank off Liberian coast following an engine room explosion in position 06.14 north by 11.40 east.

11. DOLPHIN PATRICIA/PATRICIA/WELFARE III 1976-1986

Cyprus O.N. 380918 (L.R. No. 5306784) 6,354g 2,949n
175.27 x 22.51 x 9.82 metres
Burmeister & Wain 7-cyl. 2SCSA oil engine by Société Forges et Ateliers du Creusot, Le Creusot; 8,960 BHP, 16 knots.
22.3.1958: Launched by Forges et Chantiers de la Gironde, Bordeaux (Yard No. 238) for Compagnie Francaise d'Armament Maritime, Bordeaux as SAINT THIERRY.
1958: Completed (13,631g 8,185n 20,650dwt).
1969: Sold to Northatlantic Corporation, Monrovia (Courtage et Transports S.A., Paris, managers) and renamed OLYMPIE.
1975: Managers became Transoceanic Transportation Co., Piraeus.
1976: Sold to Dolphin Shipping Co. Ltd., Limassol (Traghetti del Mediterraneo S.p.a. (Spiro P. Magliveras), Genoa, managers) and renamed DOLPHIN PATRICIA.
27.2.1977: Arrived Bacini Siciliana S.p.a., Palermo for conversion to ro-ro.
1979: Sold to Rivadeluna Navigation Co. Ltd., Limassol (Mediterranean and Overseas Shipping Agencies S.p.a. (Fotis G. Poulides), Genoa, managers) and renamed PATRICIA.
1982: Sold to Transport Services Co. Inc., Panama (Unifida S.A., Lugano, managers) and renamed WELFARE III.
1982: Provided with additional deck for vehicles.
24.11.1986: Arrived at Kaohsiung.
4.12.1986: Demolition commenced by Sun Hua Enterprise Co. Ltd.

Dolphin Lucia (above) and as *Welcome* (below). *[Both: Fotoflite incorporating Skyfotos]*

A SHIP PHOTOGRAPHER'S PARADISE
Ian Farquhar

Most ship photographers have to adapt to the circumstances of their location. They cannot readily hop off to vantage points like Prospect Point in Vancouver; North Head at the entrance to Sydney harbour; or sit on the banks of the Kiel Canal; the New Waterway, Rotterdam; or at Walsoorden on the banks of the Scheldt. They cannot savour the sparkling clear air of Cape Town; enjoy the splendid mix of shipping through the Bosphorous; or even hire a bumboat in Singapore and photograph forty to sixty different ships every hour.

Invariably the circumstances are such that the port area is effectively tucked away behind miles of security fences. Even if you can reach the wharves, there is often a troublesome background to the photo in the frame, the sun is shining on you rather than your quarry and you are obliged to use your telephoto lens at its limit. In many instances enthusiasts are limited to only the one spot in their port, a factor which greatly restricts their photographic skills. Often there is tug in the foreground or cranes in the background.

One port which is better endowed than most for ship photography is Otago in southern New Zealand. A smidgin over half the distance between the Equator and the South Pole, it is probably the southernmost liner port in the world. The largest container ships in the New Zealand trade regularly sail finally from Port Chalmers, and travel south along the 50th parallel around Cape Horn to Europe, literally following the old sailing ship routes of the nineteenth century. It is by far the most distant liner port in

the huge circle of ports from Africa, Arabian Gulf, India, South East and Northern Asia and Australia which have container feeder services into Singapore, Tanjung Pelepas and Hong Kong.

Port Otago has an eight-kilometre dredged channel from the open sea to the deepwater berthage system of Port Chalmers within the Lower Harbour, and then there is a further dredged channel of twelve kilometres in the Upper Harbour from Port Chalmers to the Dunedin wharves - Dunedin being the city served by the port. The changing tidal scour does much of the actual dredging! The channel winds itself along the northern edge of the two harbours. Ship photographers do not really have to go near the actual wharves: they can photograph ships underway at eight or nine vantage ports at an elevation above the shipping channel. Several of the spots provide a photographic result like that of an aerial view and enthusiasts can usually choose a position to suit the angle of the sun. The prime location is Pulling Point on a high bluff overlooking the shipping channel and when a new or distinctive vessel is moving, up to ten photographers can be seen at this spot. The main disadvantage for ship photography is that there are only about five hundred ship calls per annum and as the port operates over 24 hours, seven days a week, some 30% of the ship movements occur in the hours of darkness.

In the following examples, I provide some views of shipping in my 'home port' of Otago.

COLUMBUS OLIVOS
Swan Hunter Shipbuilders Ltd., Walker Shipyard, Newcastle-on-Tyne; 1980, 18,140gt, 176metres
Lengthened by Flender Werft, Lubeck; 1986, 23,291gt, 202.17metres
Two 6-cyl. 2SCSA B&W-type oil engines by Harland & Wolff Ltd., Belfast; 20,500 BHP
Early morning sun catches *Columbus Olivos* as she enters Otago Harbour in April 1998. This was her first visit to what originally was her 'name' port, as the vessel was built in 1980 as the *Dunedin* for Shaw, Savill and Albion - the first cellular container ship owned by the company. She was built for a joint service with *Willowbank* (Bank Line) and *New Zealand Caribbean* (Shipping Corporation of New Zealand) from Australia and New Zealand, initially to Caribbean and US Gulf ports and then serving North America by a land bridge through Oakland and Long Beach. Dunedin was a significant name for her owners as it was the Albion Line sailing ship *Dunedin* which carried the first cargo of frozen meat from Port Chalmers to London in 1882 - an event which dramatically enlarged New Zealand's overseas trade. Shaw, Savill sold *Dunedin* to Hamburg-Sud in 1986. She was lengthened and her container holds widened at Lubeck. She re-entered service as the *Monte Pascaol* on the

Hamburg company's South American service. Renamed *Columbus Olivos* in 1990, ownership passed to Egon Oldendorff under the Liberian flag. She reverted to *Monte Pascaol* in 1996 when she was sold to the Vlasov Group. Renamed once more *Columbus Olivos* in 1997, she was the *Alianca Hamburgo* in 1997 and 1998, initially under the Brazilian

flag then Bahamian. She then reverted to *Columbus Olivos* and throughout the entire period from 1986 to 2001 she remained under charter to Hamburg Sud/Columbus Lines. She has just taken her eighth change of name (and her sixth registry) being renamed *MSC Jessica*, still within the Vlasov Group.

SWITZERLAND

Swan, Hunter and Wigham Richardson Ltd., Wallsend; 1955, 15,833gt, 162.39 metres
Two 6-cyl 2SCSA Doxford oil engines by Wallsend Slipway Engineers Ltd., Wallsend, 13,200 BHP

As the passengers line the decks of the *Switzerland* as she leaves Port Chambers in 1998, few would be aware that the vessel had previously travelled over the same channel thirty years before as the Port Line refrigerated cargo liner *Port Sydney*. Both the *Port Sydney* and her sister ship *Port Melbourne* were sold in 1972 to J.C. Carras and Sons for operation under the Greek flag with *Port Sydney* being renamed *Akrotiri Express*. The advent of containerisation had seen the two ships sold well before their economic life was over. In 1975 she and her sister were converted to cruise liners at the Chalkis shipyard in Greece. Renamed *Daphne* she was mainly employed on short cruises around the Mediterranean and Black Seas. Under Carras ownership she was chartered to Flotto Lauro for one season and then, after five years under charter to Costa Cruises of Italy, that company purchased *Daphne* in 1984. In 1990 she was sold to Prestige Cruises of Monaco. She took her present name in 1990 when ownership passed to Leisure Cruises of Switzerland. When completed as a cargo liner she had capacity for the equivalent of 185,000 carcasses of lamb and 10,000 bales of wool but as a luxury cruise liner, albeit elderly, she can carry 503 passengers.

MARCO POLO

VEB Mathias-Thesen-Werft, Wismar; 1965, 22,080gt, 176.28 metres
Two 6-cyl. 2SCSA Sulzer diesels by H. Cegielski Zaklady Przemyslu Metlowego, Poznan; 21,000 BHP.

The *Marco Polo* spent the first 26 years of her life as the Russian passenger liner *Aleksandr Pushkin*. For much of this time she was employed cruising in the summer months and laid-up through winter. She was sold to Orient Lines of London in 1991 and then spent the next 28 months being stripped down to her main deck and entirely rebuilt at a cost of $US 80 million. Now able to carry 850 passengers compared with 700 to 750 under the Russian flag, *Marco Polo* has become well known in New Zealand waters as each year from 1994 she has operated 12-day cruises around the New Zealand coast, calling at several ports as well as the Marlborough Sounds and Milford, Thompson and Doubtful Sounds on the West Coast. She was the first foreign flag vessel to be approved for solely New Zealand cruising. As her hull was strengthened for navigation in ice she has also made many cruises to Antarctic waters, being fitted with a helipad, zodiacs and semi-enclosed lifeboats for shore excursions.

GRAND ORCHID
Jiangnan Shipyard (Group) Co. Ltd., Shanghai; 1996, 27,610gt, 45,513dwt, 190.0 metres
6-cyl. 2SCSA Sulzer-type oil engine by Shanghai Diesel Engine works, Shanghai; 11,583 BHP

Grand Orchid is seen moving towards Port Chalmers before passing through the half-way islands on the channel to Dunedin. One of the larger dry cargo vessels to visit Dunedin, *Grand Orchid* has a complicated ownership typical of many bulk carriers in that her owners are Lasco Shipping of Portland, Oregon but she is registered in the ownership of Trans-Pacific Shipping Company of Port Vila, Vanuatu - a port she is unlikely ever to visit. On this voyage *Grand Orchid* is on charter to a fertiliser company, carrying sulphur and potash from Vancouver.

KAKARIKI
Stocnia Szczecinska S.A., Szczecin, 1999, 27,795gt, 46,724dwt, 183.0 metres
Two 6-cyl 2SCSA Sulzer-type oil engines by Stocnia Szczecinska S.A., Szczecin, 12,018 BHP

Kakariki (the name of a New Zealand native bird) was specially designed for the distribution of petroleum products, including bitumen, around the New Zealand coast. Carrying refined product from the Marsden Point refinery, or heavy oil for refining from New Plymouth to Marsden Point, *Kakariki* is owned by Coastal Tankers Ltd., a consortium of the Shell, Mobil, BP and Caltex oil companies. She is equipped with a Schilling rudder which can be positioned ninety degrees to port or starboard, making the vessel very manoeuvrable in restricted port areas. The photograph shows *Kakariki* in the Upper Harbour with the extinct volcano, Harbour Cone, in the background. Apart from Dunedin, ports regularly visited are Marsden Point, Napier, Wellington, Lyttelton, Timaru, Bluff, Nelson and New Plymouth.

SKULPTORS TOMSKIS

Aalborg Vaerft A/S, Aalborg, 1986, 9,952gt, 138.20 metres
Two 6-cyl 2SCSA B & W-type oil engines by Bryansk Engineering Works, Bryansk, 13,050 BHP

Under long-term charter to Lauritzen Reefers, the *Skulptors Tomskis* leaves Dunedin for Europe in 1995 with a full cargo of apples. She was one of a trio of fast (20.3 knots) refrigerated ships built at the Lauritzen-controlled Aalborg shipyard in Denmark for Morflot but, following the break-up of the Government-controlled shipping fleets in the USSR, she was transferred to the Latvian Shipping Company of Riga in 1991. She also took her present name in 1991, having been completed as *Skulptor Tomskiy*. In 1994

ownership was transferred to S. Tomkis Shipping Co. Ltd., with registration under the Cypriot flag. She came under Maltese registry in 2000.

NORA MAERSK

China Shipbuilding Corporation, Kaohsiung; 2000, 27,733gt
Two 6-cyl. 2SCSA Sulzer-type oil engines by China Shipbuilding Corporation, Kaohsiung, 38,539 BHP

Outward bound from the southernmost port in the world at which Maersk Sealand container vessels call, the 21.8 knot *Nora Maersk* is one of four identical vessels built in Taiwan during 2000 specifically for the relay service from New Zealand to Singapore. With the company's withdrawal from Singapore the vessels

are now exchanging their containers at the Malaysian port of Tanjung Pelepas. Maersk Line entered the New Zealand trade in 1997 and the four new ships each have capacity for the equivalent of 2,240 TEUs. On the passage from New Zealand the vessels carry a high percentage of refrigerated cargo, with meat, dairy produce, fish, and apples being the main commodities. Much of this cargo is transshipped to other international destinations by the larger Maersk Sealand vessels coming through Tanjung Pelepas from the Far East. Under the Danish International Registry, the vessels are registered at ports in Denmark at which they are often too large to call. *Nora Maersk* is registered at Aabenraa.

FRED. OLSEN CRUISE SHIPS *(continued from page 91)* which would serve no less than three, quite different, purposes. In the summer months, she would run as a car ferry for the Bergen Line on their express route between Bergen and the Tyne. But she could be converted for wintertime use by Olsens as a fruit-carrier between the Canaries and London. At the same time, these voyages could be marketed in Britain as a regular cruise service to the islands, similar to those run for many years by the fruit ships of the Yeoward and Aznar Lines. This would be Olsens' first serious venture into the cruise business.

When in Bergen Line service, the new ship would be known as the *Jupiter*; and when running for Olsens she would be called *Black Watch*. Most unusually, she was thus officially registered in two names. At the same time, Olsens ordered a sister ship, *Black Prince*, entirely for themselves. During the Summer, she would run in their

'pendulum service' – alternating sailings between Kristiansand and Harwich and between Kristiansand and Amsterdam – and in winter she would join her sister on the Canary Islands route. The two ships were completed in 1966. In 1970, with Olsens about to introduce a larger vessel, the Bergen Line bought a share in *Black Prince* under a similar arrangement to that involving her sister. Henceforth, she too had twin names: *Black Prince* and *Venus*. For twenty years, the two ships were enormously successful.

The ingenious design of *Black Watch* and *Black Prince* was largely the work of Olsens' own technical department, under Mr. John Johnsen. They had a reputation for innovative thinking, especially in respect of cargo-handling methods, where they were enthusiasts for palletisation. Tomatoes and other produce were piled on pallets and stowed in cooled holds, having been loaded

Ships with two names. Running for Bergen Line in summer her name was *Jupiter*, as seen left at North Shields, and when working for Olsens in the winter she was *Black Watch* (below). *[Left: Malcolm Donnelly; below: Fotoflite incorporating Skyfotos]*
Venus, seen opposite top at North Shields running for Bergen Line, and opposite below in Olsen service as *Black Prince*. *[Top: Malcolm Donnelly, lower: Fotoflite incorporating Skyfotos]*

through ports in the ship's side. The operation was accomplished by a system of conveyor belts and about 40 purpose-built fork lift trucks, operating both ashore and aboard. In London, a new, specially-designed terminal was built at Millwall Dock, near the site of the present London Arena. The aim was to unload and load the ships in just six hours. Inevitably, in the industrial climate of the times, there was opposition from the dockers and their union but the terminal was brought into operation in 1970.

When the ships were to operate as ferries, large parts of the cargo space were quickly converted into car decks, loaded over a stern ramp. There was a similar adaptability about the passenger quarters. On the North Sea routes each ship could carry up to 591 passengers, mainly in single and double cabins, some of them quite small but each having its own private facilities. There were also a few couchette seats. As cruise ships, however, the sisters were limited to 370 passengers. The ferry cafeteria

Blenheim of 1970 in the New Waterway 30th July 1973.

was converted into a high-class restaurant simply by shuttering off the business end of the room. The complete twice-yearly conversion could be accomplished in just 48 hours, including painting new names on bow and stern and either the Fred. Olsen or the Bergen Line flag on both sides of the funnel. The ships were instantly recognisable, not only because of their beautiful bow bronzes but because of their bay window-shaped bridge fronts and the unusual helmet-like funnels, again designed to keep smoke and soot off the after decks. (It has to be said that, in my own experience, they have not always been effective.) The ships were given ice-strengthened hulls and such modern appurtenances as bulbous bows, stabilisers, controllable pitch propellers and side thrusters.

It was a time when German yards were very active in the ferry market and the contract to build the two ships went to the Lübecker Flender Werke. There is no doubt that they produced two exceptionally sturdy vessels. Power came from two Pielstick medium-speed V18-cylinder diesel engines. On *Black Prince*, except for a serious breakdown in 1988, these have given yeoman service and have now covered an enormous mileage.

Blenheim: a problem child

Fred. Olsen's Canary Islands cruise service, latterly with a call at Madeira, soon gained an enthusiastic following among middle-aged, middle-class, middle-brow British passengers. With the Millwall terminal about to become operational, it was possible for the company to contemplate a larger ship. Basically a lengthened version of the *Black Watch* and *Black Prince* (490 ft. 1in. long, as against 464 ft. 8ins.), the new vessel revived the name *Blenheim*. She was built at the John Brown yard at Clydebank, which by the time the ship was completed had become part of Upper Clyde Shipbuilders. In order to win the contract, which they needed in order to keep their fitting-out department going, they quoted a low price of £4 million and guaranteed a firm delivery date of February 1970. This rash promise was to cause great grief all round.

Labour disputes and other problems delayed the launch until the 10th January 1970. It cannot have been a cordial occasion. Late delivery was very inconvenient and expensive for Olsens who had to charter another ship to deputise for the *Blenheim* and, even so, had to divert passengers to other routes or send them by air. Upper Clyde Shipbuilders were faced with the prospect of paying a large amount of compensation. They made it known that

the *Blenheim* would almost certainly be the last fully-fledged passenger ship to come from the Clydebank yard – which in its time had built such great liners as *Lusitania, Aquitania, Queen Mary* and the recently completed *Queen Elizabeth 2*.

The forward half of the *Blenheim* was an almost exact replica of the two earlier ships, but the after section was rather longer. Her official tonnage was 10,420 gross. She had several bouts of trouble with her engines (Pielsticks built by Crossley-Premier) and sometimes found it difficult to keep up to schedule. Nevertheless, she was in other ways a fine ship and her extra capacity, especially for cargo, was useful. With three vessels now available, the Canary Islands service could be expanded and Olsens now ran *Black Prince* out of Rotterdam, catering for Dutch and German cruise passengers but retaining her English name.

Three years later, they took delivery of another cruise-ferry – but, ironically, she never wore Fred. Olsen colours while serving as a cruise ship, although she had a very useful career with the company as a ferry. The *Bolero*, 11,344 gross tons, was one of a number of similar ships built by the Dubigeon-Normandie yard at Nantes for various companies. They had a very distinctive appearance with a pair of huge, side-by-side funnels placed well aft. Perhaps the best-known of this class of near-sisters is the one which now sails as Festival Cruises' *The Azur*. The *Bolero* was chartered to the Swedish company Lion Ferry to replace the *Prince of Fundy* on the summer service between Portland, Maine and Yarmouth, Nova Scotia and cruised the Caribbean in winter. She remained with Lion Ferry (and Commodore Cruise Line) for nearly four years before returning to Europe to take her place in Olsens' own ferry services.

Black Prince/Venus was out of action for much of the summer of 1973 after striking an underwater object at Trondheim in May of that year, a serious blow for the Bergen Line, but on the whole *Black Prince, Black Watch* and *Blenheim* continued to run very successfully. In the late 1970s, one or other of them would work the Tyne to Oslo route during the summer months. By the early 1980s, however, there were big changes in the ferry industry in northern Europe. The grand old Danish company DFDS began an aggressive expansion not only in Europe but also, unsuccessfully, in the US market. The effect on the Olsen fleet was two-fold. In late 1981, DFDS announced the take-over of the Olsen and Bergen Line North Sea ferry

Bolero. [Peter Newall collection]

services and time-chartered *Black Prince* and *Black Watch*. They returned them to Olsen each winter, however, for the Canary Islands season. Secondly, the *Blenheim* was bought outright by DFDS who re-named her *Scandinavian Sea* and re-fitted her for short cruises out of Port Canaveral in Florida for their new Scandinavian World Cruises subsidiary. The *Blenheim* was British-flagged and her British crew were naturally unhappy about her sale. She was making a Mediterranean cruise when the news broke and they went on strike at Gibraltar. When she finally returned to Plymouth, they staged an occupation. Eventually, redundancy terms were agreed.

Black Prince rejuvenated

The arrangement between Olsens and the Bergen Line expired after twenty years and in 1986 the *Black Watch* became entirely owned by the Bergen Line, who promptly sold her to the new Norway Line. Olsens became the sole owners of *Black Prince* and sent her to the Wärtsilä yard in Finland for conversion into a full-time cruise ship. Her passenger capacity was increased to 527 after rearrangement of the existing accommodation and the addition of a further 125 cabins on what had formerly been the car deck. The public rooms were refurbished and a new two-deck high lounge was constructed. The most notable change, however, was the installation of a 'marina park' in the aperture hitherto occupied by the stern ramp. Described as a 'floating leisure centre', this could be floated out when the ship was at anchor in calm waters and provided facilities for a variety of water sports. It had been designed by MacGregor-Navire and the contract stipulated that they would not produce anything similar for other owners within a stated period.

Olsens now tried to attract a younger, trendier, more active clientele to the ship. In an effort to make her even more distinctive, her hull was adorned with strange artwork and a pair of small, non-functioning sails could be erected on the after deck when she was in port! The 'new' *Black Prince* re-entered service in 1987, but with rather limited success. After several seasons based variously in

Southampton, the Mediterranean, northern Europe and Madeira, she was withdrawn from the cruise market and introduced into a new ferry service between Copenhagen and Gothenburg. Registered in the Philippines and with an international crew, she aroused vigorous opposition from the Danish and Swedish unions. Quickly, Olsens abandoned the attempt and the *Black Prince* became a cruise ship again, but now aimed once more at her traditional middle-aged market. Usually sailing out of British ports, mainly Dover, she has again attracted a loyal following. In recent years, she has occasionally ventured beyond her old haunts, making some long winter cruises to the Caribbean, the Amazon and Africa.

Larger cruise ships

The success of the reborn *Black Prince* encouraged Olsens to seek another, larger cruise ship. After a long search, they bought the 28,221-ton *Star Odyssey* in 1996. They had her refitted to carry 830 passengers and revived the favourite name of *Black Watch* for her. There was a certain irony about this purchase. The ship had belonged to the Royal Cruise Line, part of the Kloster group. The Klosters were another of the big Oslo shipping dynasties and in order to obtain the ship Olsens had to buy her from a third party. She had been a very significant vessel in the history of the cruise trade. Built in 1972, she had been the *Royal Viking Star,* one of the trio of ships with which a consortium of Norwegian owners, including the Bergen Line, had set up the Royal Viking Line. Royal Viking had been vastly influential in the cruise industry. Together with the Royal Caribbean Line (also Norwegian) and the Kloster-owned Norwegian Caribbean Line, they had been largely responsible for the revival of deep-sea passenger shipping after the collapse of the ocean liner trades due to the incursions of the jet aeroplane in the late 1950s and 1960s. Their ships were among the earliest to establish the modern cruise ship profile – short, raked bow; superstructure spread along much of the length of the hull; engines towards the stern. They did not, though, have the piled-up look of many later examples of the species. In

The latest *Black Watch* seen passing Gibraltar (opposite) and against a dramatic sky at Southampton on 10th November 1996 (left). Her origins as a Royal Viking Line ship are apparent. *[Opposite: Fotoflite incorporating Skyfotos, left: John Adams]*

Fred. Olsen's latest acquisition, *Braemar*, at Dover in August 2001 (bottom). *[Ambrose Greenway]*

1984, the Royal Viking Line was purchased by Klosters and in later years the *Royal Viking Star* was transferred to other companies within the group.

The purchase of this important ship was not at first a happy move by Olsens. She was plagued by expensive engine problems, which caused her to miss her introductory date with the press and the travel trade at Dover and to cut short a long, round-Africa cruise. Once the problems were overcome, however, she gradually established herself in the British market. She offers a mixture of cruises out of British ports and from more distant places which take her not only to the Baltic and the Mediterranean but also to such parts as the Far East, southern Asia and North and South America.

With the cruise market still expanding, Fred. Olsen Cruise Lines (as this part of the Olsen empire was now known) began to eye further vessels ripe for purchase.

Early in 2001, they found their ship. The 19,089-ton, 800-passenger *Crown Dynasty* had been built in Spain in 1993 and was therefore more modern than the existing pair. Her career has been somewhat chequered but, nevertheless, she has been a well-regarded ship. The collapse of her latest owners, the Commodore Cruise Line group, gave Olsens their opportunity. They have given her yet another traditional Olsen name, *Braemar* and, fittingly, some of her public rooms have been refurnished with a Scottish touch. She started cruising out of Dover and Southampton in August 2001.

In an era when the cruise business has experienced a 'big bang', which has left it dominated by a few huge combines, the family-owned Fred. Olsen Cruise Lines have survived and apparently prospered, concentrating on the British market which they know so well.

BANK LINE IN COLOUR

Weirbank (above) was the twelth of the Doxford-built 12,000 ton deadweight series and might, more appropriately, have been named *Wearbank*. Seen here sailing from Liverpool in June 1975, she was sold to Greek interests three years later. As *Saronic Sky,* she was declared a constructive total loss in 1980 after sustaining severe collision damage during a storm at Oran and was broken up at Gadani Beach the following year. [Paul Boot]

The singular styling of *Lossiebank* (below) marked the late metamorphosis of the design of this Harland and Wolff series. After 16 years in Bank's service she too was acquired by Greeks, becoming *Evoicos Gulf* in 1979. Her active career ended in 1982 and after spending the next three years laid up at Piraeus, she was broken up at Alang. [D. Salisbury]

Riding at anchor on an unusually fine Spring Bank Holiday Monday afternoon in 1978, *Hollybank* (left, opposite) presents another angle on her distinctive profile as she awaits the tide prior to docking at Liverpool. She appears to be in exemplary condition - even the flags and ensign look remarkably fresh - yet the following year she was to be sold and she would effectively make her last trading voyage just two years later. *[Paul Boot]*

Taybank (above) was the first of the larger developments of the earlier Doxford series. She shared the same styling of the superstructure with the later *Hollybank,* but had two additional derricks rigged from the bridge front. Under a threatening summer sky she makes an impressive sight outward bound from Rotterdam, with the fresh anti-fouling paint suggesting a recent spell in dry-dock. Sold to Greeks in 1978, she became *Good Breeze,* later transferring to Panamanian registration. Renamed *Athos* in 1984, she arrived at Chittagong the following year for breaking. *[D. Salisbury]*

The bright new colours of the Ceylon Shipping Corporation do little to disguise the classic Harland and Wolff lines of the former *Dartbank.* Acquired by the emergent Sri Lankan company in 1975 and renamed *Lanka Keerti,* she was to give them ten years' service, passing to breakers at Gadani Beach early in 1985. Photographed in the first year of service in her new guise, *Lanka Keerti* (below) seems exceptionallly well maintained, with the light grey-painted hull highlighting the rivetted strakes. *[Paul Boot]*

THEMES AND VARIATIONS:
THE DEVELOPMENT OF POST-WAR BANK LINE CARGO SHIPS PART 2
Paul Boot

Both Doxford and Harland and Wolff completed the final examples in each of their series of 12,000 ton deadweight vessels during 1964, with Harland's *Weybank* entering service in March, five months ahead of the Sunderland-built *Sprucebank*. Whilst Doxford had introduced a multitude of variations during the course of the construction of the 21 vessels that comprised their group, Harland had eschewed this policy of innovation and refinement. No doubt the construction of five passenger ships during this same period, which included the innovative *Canberra* for P. & O., had kept the drawing office preoccupied with more important matters. Thus, the first twelve ships of the Harland group, commencing with *Cloverbank* built in 1957, were to all intents and purposes identical. But, after five years of this remarkable uniformity, the builders must have felt the need for a change, no matter how minor. *Springbank*, commissioned in January 1962, as well as her later twin, *Olivebank*, sported a tapered funnel and, as with *Sprucebank*, this small difference in detail imparted a significant effect on the overall appearance, giving them a more purposeful look. This pair also initiated the upgrading of the heavy-lift capabilities which, at 50 tons, was now double the previous capacity. Though still a comparatively modest

figure, it was adequate for the trades within which these ships were generally employed. *Lossiebank*, which did not enter service until well over a year later, in July 1963, after a slightly prolonged period fitting out, continued the theme but differed in a number of respects. Fore and main top masts gave way to an enlarged signal mast carrying the radar scanner on top of the bridge - some two years after Doxfords had adopted this same arrangement. Similarly, a single mast was fitted between the second and third hatches, in lieu of the twin posts installed in the earlier ships. More spacious accommodation for the chief engineer and officers was afforded by the full width extension of the superstructure at the fore end of the boat deck to which a minor, but noticeable feature, was the supporting raked stanchions. If only in these details, *Lossiebank* was unique and it could be said that, alone amongst her Harland peers, she had no equals. Having finally broken the mould, *Roybank* and *Weybank,* the final exponents of this class, were furnished with a completely restyled superstructure, which featured a well proportioned modish funnel combined with the signal mast. At the stern, however, tradition lingered on with the large Asian crew quartered in the raised poop.

The twelve ships delivered by Harland and Wolff between 1957 and 1961 were a true series production design and might well have all been built from the same set of drawings. Pictured here on the New Waterway on 13th September 1969, *Pinebank,* the ninth in this group, was sold off in 1976, as were two of her sisters, to a London based organisation. Placed under the Liberian flag as *Newark,* she lasted barely a year. After stranding off Tripoli in November 1977, she was found to be beyond economical repair and the following year she was towed to Spanish breakers. *[World Ship Photo Library]*

Weybank (opposite page) was the last of this extended Harland-built group to enter service in 1964 and, with her twin sister *Roybank,* differed markedly from the earlier examples in the styling of the superstructure and funnel. Both sisters were sold in 1979; a year which saw no less than 15 ships disposed of by the company.

Weybank's new Taiwanese-based owners put her under the Panamanian flag as *Golden Nigeria,* keeping her until 1984 when she was broken up at Kaohsiung. In better times, *Weybank* is seen arriving at Liverpool, at the beginning of a voyage charter to Harrison Line in October 1975. *[Paul Boot]*

The Harland & Wolff Vessels
Types HW 1 – HW 3

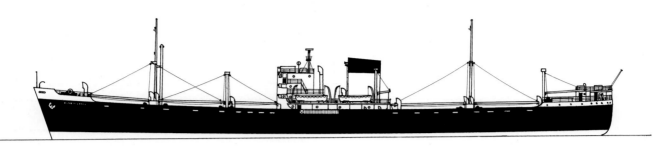

Types HW1/1
& HW1/2

BEAVERBANK

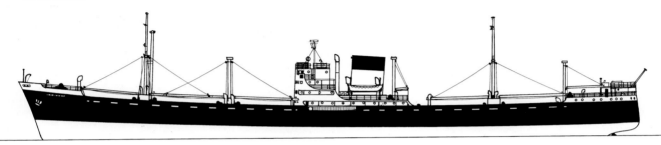

Types HW2/a
HW2/b *similar, except for funnel (as HW2/c)*

CLOVERBANK

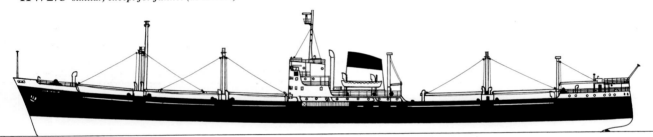

Type HW2/c

LOSSIEBANK

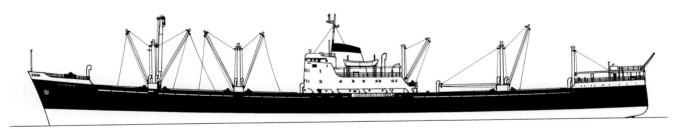

Type HW2/d

ROYBANK

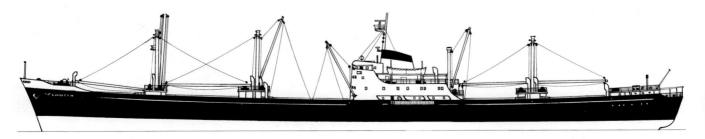

Type HW3

HAZELBANK

Vessels built by Harland and Wolff Ltd.
Belfast

Type HW1/1

Length (o.a.): 450'   Breadth: 59'4'''   Main engine: H&W-B&W 6-cyl. opposed piston

	Completed	Tonnage Gross	Tonnage Deadweight	Notes Distinguishing features / drawing reference
BEAVERBANK	2.1953	5,690*	8,983*	
NESSBANK	6.1953	5,690*	8,983*	
FLEETBANK	10.1953	5,690*	8.967*	

Type HW1/2

Length (o.a.): 455'   Breadth: 59' 4" (a) / 59' 3" (b)   Main engine: H&W-B&W 6-cyl. opposed piston

	Completed	Gross	Deadweight	
CEDARBANK	1 1955	5,671*	-	(a)
FOYLEBANK	8.1955	5,671*	-	(b)
LAGANBANK	10.1955	5,671*	-	(b)

Type HW2

Length (o.a.): 483"   Breadth: 62' 9"   Main engine: H&W-B&W 6-cyl. opposed piston (turbocharged)

	Completed	Gross	Deadweight	Drawing Reference	
CLOVERBANK	3.1957	6,459*	10,277*	HW2/a	
CRESTBANK	6.1957	6,459*	10,277*	HW2/a	
CARRONBANK	9.1957	6,461*	10,277*	HW2/a	
DARTBANK	1.1958	6,461*	10,277*	HW2/a	
GARRYBANK	4.1958	8,694	12,100	HW2/a	
MINCHBANK	9.1958	8,694	12,288	HW2/a	
ROSEBANK	4.1959	8,694	12,317	HW2/a	
ASHBANK	5.1959	8,694	12,336	HW2/a	
PINEBANK	9.1959	6,452*	10,147*	HW2/a	
ELMBANK	4.1960	6,449*	10,107*	HW2/a	
AVONBANK	1.1961	6,443*	10,107*	HW2/a	
LEVERNBANK	8.1961	6,443*	10,182*	HW2/a	
SPRINGBANK	1.1962	6,461*	10,162*	(HW2/b)	Hull and superstructure as HW2/a; funnel as HW2/c
OLIVEBANK	4.1962	8,694	12,336	(HW2/b)	Hull and superstructure as HW2/a; funnel as HW2/c
LOSSIEBANK	7.1963	6,433*	10,374*	HW2/c	
ROYBANK	10.1963	6,526*	12,257	HW2/d	
WEYBANK	3.1964	6,527*	10,437*	HW2/d	

Type HW3

Length (o.a.): 513'   Breadth: 67' 8"   Main engine: H&W-B&W 6-cyl. opposed piston (turbocharged)

	Completed	Gross	Deadweight	
HAZELBANK	5.1964	10,507	15,209	
IRISBANK	10.1964	10,526	15,411	
NAIRNBANK	7.1966	10,363	15,377	
MAPLEBANK	8.1967	10,365	15,385	
GOWANBANK	1.1968	10,370	15,916	

	*	*	Tonnages measured as completed as an open shelterdecker

General Note   The type designations are not official and have been adopted solely for the purposes of this article

This profile view of *Springbank* in ballast shows how just a small change to the shape of the funnel gave three ships in this group a different character to the first 12 The distinctive cruiser stern is also well evident.

She was just one of a dozen sold off during the course of 1978. Renamed *Global Med* by her new owners, this was changed to *Terrie U* the following year, possibly for the duration of a charter, but reverted to *Global Med*

in 1980. Four years later she arrived at Kaohsiung to provide yet another contribution to Taiwan's then insatiable demand for scrap metal. *[M.Cranfield]*

Marabank and her sister *Speybank* embodied many of the features of Swan, Hunter's stillborn concept for a standard ship. Despite them being the only two ships to be powered by Sulzer diesels, as well as having other non-standard details, they seem to have integrated well into the fleet. Both were sold off in 1978, taking the very similar colours of the Good Faith Shipping Co. S.A.; managers of a host of single ship companies controlled by Nikolaos Frangos. *Marabank* became *Good Lady* and lasted until 1985 when she was despatched to the breakers at Chittagong. *[J. Krayenbosch/P. Boot]*

Between them, these two yards had delivered 38 ships, with one having entered service on average every ten weeks during the seven year construction period. In the midst of all this activity though, two strangers had entered the camp.

Something of a standard

In the face of ever increasing competition from foreign yards, many shipbuilders were drawing up plans for standard ship designs in the early 'sixties. Some produced imposing portfolios of a range of types, most of which progressed no further than the artists' impressions. Throughout these proposed schemes ran a common theme; a 12-14,000 ton deadweight, basic general cargo ship that could be offered at a price that would be attractive to the operators of ageing Liberties and other superannuated wartime built workhorses. Amongst these proposals, the Swan Hunter Group presented their 'Efficiency Class' design which, it was intended, would be built at each of its yards. Their Wallsend yard, more noted for producing tankers, had insufficient experience in building this type of cargo ship and, it would seem, Swans sought to acquire the expertise by offering extremely attractive prices; an offer which Weir's could not resist. Two very individual vessels resulted: *Speybank* handed over in June 1962, and *Marabank* in February 1963. They were very different in appearance from either the Doxford or Harland designs and incorporated some of the features drawn from the proposed 'Efficiency Class' design; most notably an inset superstructure with extended bridge wings and a pronounced rake to the fore, as well as widely splayed bipod masts. Together with the extended forecastle encompassing the hatchway to the No.1 hold, the design had a decidedly 'un British' look about it. The five-cylinder, Wallsend-built, Sulzer engine was also of the type proposed for the 'Efficiency Class'. One feature which was certainly not appreciated by those who sailed on these

ships, was the squat funnel incorporated into the bridge house. Nicely proportioned it may have been, but efficient it was not, causing the exhaust fumes to swirl around the boat and after decks, where they were drawn into the accommodation by the air-conditioning system, thus somewhat negating this particular advancement. Surprisingly, although Andrew Weir's initial acquisition, the iron barque *Willowbank,* had been built by Swan's predecessors, these were the first ships to be actually ordered from them. They were not to be the last, however, and, but a few years on, these builders would make a more significant contribution to the fleet.

By now, the company had determined a requirement for a larger ship than these two 12,000 ton deadweight classes and Doxfords completed the forerunner of a new 15,000 ton deadweight design almost a year before the original series had run its full course. This was little more than a moderately enlarged version of the earlier design, with the hull now twenty feet longer overall and five feet greater in beam. It is interesting to note that, even at this late date, riveting was still favoured for certain of the more highly stressed connections in the hull; in particular the bilge and 'midships sheerstrakes. *Taybank,* delivered in December 1963 and *Tweedbank* just weeks later in January, premièred the styling of the funnel and superstructure that would be applied to the last two variants of the original series, *Hollybank* and *Sprucebank,* as recorded earlier. Otherwise, only the MacGregor type hatch covers, together with the concomitant raised winch-houses, distinguished these two 'big sisters' from their siblings. In the following pair, however, *Beechbank* and *Ernebank* - both completed during 1964 - the almost totally enclosed bridge deck and the downwardly angled wheelhouse windows displayed what was to be the final phase in the evolution of the superstructure. Yet two further, and even larger, versions were built a couple of years later: *Shirrabank* delivered in 1966 and *Teviotbank* in 1967. Apart from their dimensions,

Tweedbank was one of no less than five Banks that passed to Good Faith Shipping Co. S.A., during 1978-79 (including *Marabank* and *Taybank*). The newest of these five, her time in their fleet was to be the shortest. Under the slightly absurd name of *Good Lion*, she went aground at Corcubion, in Finisterre Bay, a few days before Christmas in 1983, on a voyage from Iran to Bremen. Abandoned by her crew, she was subsequently declared a constructive total loss. *[Fotoflite, incorporating Skyfotos]*

these were all but identical in appearance to the preceding pair, but differed significantly in their main machinery, being equipped with the new Doxford 'J' type engine. With a continuous service output of 10,800 BHP, this six-cylinder version produced over 50% greater power than the previous 'P' type engine and enabled these two vessels to comfortably operate at a service speed of 17 knots.

The 'J' type engine was to be the pinnacle of half a century's development of the Doxford opposed-piston designs. There were to be no further new models, no more major advancements. Less than twenty years later, the company would cease engine production for ever.

Ernebank was one of the later pair of the Doxford built, 15,000 ton deadweight, quartet and thus represented the penultimate development in this series.

Another casualty of the programme of mass disposals during 1979, *Ernebank* became the quaintly named *Family Unity*, owned by the eponymous Family Unity Shipping Co. S.A. Sold on in 1982, she moved to Bangladesh ownership as the *Bengal Star* and was broken up in that country, at Chittagong, in January 1988.

The Erne, one of the principal rivers of northern Ireland, was a perverse choice for one of the Sunderland built 'banks'. Together with a few other inappropriate examples, this suggests that naming seems to have become a rather arbitrary exercise at times. In the main, names were drawn from the long, established list that went back to the company's origins. Themed mainly on trees and British rivers, only the Fishbank class saw the introduction of some new, if not always prosaic, appellations.

Irisbank was the second of this last group of five cargo ships built by Harland and Wolff. These had a finely balanced, elegant profile that even in the mid 1960s was becoming ever more the exception. Of the five, *Irisbank* was to have the longest career by far. Sold in 1979 to Greek principals, along with her sister *Hazelbank*, she became *Oceanaut*, but was soon sold on again. Buyers were the paradoxical Government of the Democratic People's Republic of North Korea and, as *Kang Dong*, she served them for the next 14 years. In 1994, by then thirty years old, she was broken up at Alang. *[J. Krayenbosch/P. Boot]*

Harland's finale

Meanwhile, across the Irish Sea, Harland and Wolff too had the construction of a clutch of very similar sized ships in hand. *Hazelbank*, the first of a class of five, was completed in May 1964, just three months after *Weybank*, the final member of the earlier group. Although the superstructure was closely modelled on that of *Weybank* and her sister, the hull form was distinctly different. The plain, rounded cruiser stern, now without a raised poop, together with the enlarged winch houses gave these vessels a profile that had more in common with the contemporary Doxford products than their Harland forebears. Deliveries were spread over four years and *Gowanbank*, the last of this group, was handed over at the beginning of 1968. She could almost certainly claim to be one of, if not the, last conventional 'midships cargo ships to be built in the British Isles. At the onset of an era that would have little regard for the finer points of design, she and her sisters presented a poise and elegance which would not be seen again.

Teviotbank and Gowanbank marked the end of the development of each of these two series which, after over twenty years of divergent development, had now returned to a commonality of form. With the departure of the three 'Compass' -banks a couple of years previously, it also marked the conclusion of the post-war reconstruction programme.

Doxford's last 'midships cargo ship for the company was *Teviotbank*, completed in 1967. She was yet another victim of the 1979 cull of these conventional designs. After a short spell flying the Liberian flag, she returned to the British registry in 1980 under the nominal ownership of Alexander Properties Ltd. of Douglas. Little effort was expended on giving her a new identity and just a brushfull or two of white paint was all that was necessary to change the name to *Teviotban*. In 1985, during the Iran-Iraq conflict, she was towed in to Bandar Abbas after an engine breakdown, where she was later abandoned. *[P.Boot collection]*

For the first time in over fifteen years the company had no new ships on order and, moreover, no further new tonnage was to be commissioned until 1972. It was a time to stand back, review the rapidly changing scene and attempt to anticipate what the future would hold for conventional cargo carriers and especially for tramp ship operators. Like other shipowners, Bank looked carefully at the popular SD14 type that was rapidly gaining acceptance from liner companies, but concluded that, even with modifications, these would not suit their diverse and sometimes specialised requirements. In particular it was considered that a faster and larger vessel, with a partial container capability, was needed for the liner trades; both their own and in the lucrative charter market. As Harland and Wolff had by this time decided that its future lay in other directions and was no longer interested in building medium-sized cargo vessels, the two yards in the north east were to be favoured with these orders. Contracts were signed for a total of ten ships; four from Doxfords and six from Swan, Hunter. The designs from these two builders were both to be very different to their earlier constructions.

Doxfords adopted the hull form of a 16,000 ton deadweight class of which they had already built 17 examples for a variety of owners. Of what is commonly referred to as of the three-quarters aft configuration, these ships still exhibited a nice symmetry in their profile, even if the semblance of sheer was no more than an inclination of the bow and stern sections to an otherwise planar deck line. The long sweeping hances and well flared bow contrasted oddly with the transom stern, where more utilitarian shipbuilding practices had displaced the finer form of the old. Provision was made for carriage of only 144 standard 20-foot containers, with twin hatchways to Nos. 3 and 4 holds, and strengthened double bottom tanks to allow tiered stacking. Such was the growth of containerisation that this was soon to prove a far too limited capacity. By the time *Fleetbank,* the first of these ships, was completed, Wm. Doxford & Sons Ltd., had become part of the Court Shipbuilding Group. As rationalisation of the shipbuilding industry took its toll, it became Doxford and Sunderland Shipbuilding and Engineering Co. Ltd., and later lost its identity completely

The twelve members of this Doxford-built class averaged little more than 6½ years' service with the company. *Cloverbank* (above) managed eight years, which included a year on charter to the East Asiatic Co., when she ran as *Siena.* Sold in 1981 she then passed through the hands of a number of flag of convenience operators. After four years as *Colorado* under Liberian registration, she became the Panamanian *Bahia III.* In 1986 she hoisted the Cypriot flag as *Marie H,* later becoming *Marie A,* as which she arrived at Mumbai for breaking in May 1999.
[J Krayenbosch/P. Boot]

This aerial view of *Crestbank* (left) clearly shows the twin hatches provided to Nos. 3 and 4 holds, to facilitate the stowage of containers. She was acquired by Tamahine Shipping in 1986 and renamed *Tamathai.* The following year she passed to Greek interests as *Northman,* but returned to Tamahine as *Tamamima* in 1988 and is now the sole survivor of this class.

The six Swan, Hunter vessels that entered service from 1973 were to outlast their Doxford-built contemporaries by several years and some were to be the last conventional ships to operate in the company's service. *Ivybank* was retained until 1998, by then registered in the Isle of Man. Sold to an obscure company based in St. Vincent - one of several improbable maritime countries to have emerged in recent years - her new name, *Pro Pacifica*, points to the involvement of Hamburg-based managers, K.G. Reederei Roth G.m.b.H. [P.Boot]

within Sunderland Shipbuilders Ltd. In a massive investment programme, a new covered construction dock was built on the site of the old Pallion Yard and *Cedarbank*, the fifth of what had now been increased to an order for twelve ships, had the distinction of taking the new yard number 1. Yet a further six ships of a modified design were ordered in 1977. Commonly referred to as the 'Fishbank' class, these differed in having a raised deck aft and Velle type crane derricks. The resultant deep transom stern and the heavier oval section masts, with one perched uncomfortably right aft, did little for the appearance of this class.

Swan song

On the Tyne, the reorganisation of the shipyards had brought about Swan, Hunter controlling the remainder of the builders on that river and the six ships of their order were distributed around three different yards, although they were given consecutive yard numbers. *Corabank*, the first to enter service in February 1973, came from the former Readhead's yard, as did *Moraybank* nine months later and *Ivybank* in June 1974. *Forthbank* and *Clydebank* were both built at Hebburn, at what had been Hawthorn, Leslie's premises, with only *Meadowbank* coming from Swan's old yard at Wallsend. *Clydebank* was a particularly inappropriate choice of name when *Tynebank*, last used on a Readhead-built steamer sold off in 1955, would have been far more fitting. The class had much in common with

their Doxford counterparts, including a 'J' type engine, but the combination of cranes and derricks, together with a long raised quarter-deck gave them a somewhat different demeanour. Largely because of their superior deep tank capacity as well as a small, but useful refrigerated space, they were to prove the more enduring though and *Forthbank*, the last to remain in the company's service, carried their colours for twenty seven years.

But a handful of the ships sold on to other owners still exist and in an age when the general cargo vessel is rapidly becoming almost as much of an anachronism as the sailing ship, these few survivors stand out amongst the nondescript and unlovely modern creations. Andrew Weir's company is still, of course, very much in existence and maintains a regular service to the South Pacific Islands using four former Russian ro-ro ships, which were acquired in 1995 and adapted for this service. Sadly, apart from their traditional style names, these have little else to commend them.

No attempt has been made to fully chronicle the history and disposal of these ships. The World Ship Society's short history and fleet list of Bank Line, published in 1985 and now unfortunately out of print, gives a comprehensive account up to that date. 'British Tramps', by Ian Stewart, records the details of all their ships owned between 1939 and 1997 and thus provides a more up to date, but selective, listing.

With the decks stacked high with containers, *Meadowbank* has been reduced to a supporting role in the new era of cargo handling.

After spending a year on charter as *Toana Niugini,* she was the second of the class to be sold, becoming *Pro Atlantica* in 1987 under the Cypriot flag, but managed by Roth's Pro Line Ltd. & Co. G.m.b.H. She did well to sail into the new millennium, being broken up in China in July 2000.

Vessels built by Wm. Doxford and Sunderland Ltd., *(D&S)* and Sunderland Shipbuilders Ltd. *(Sund)*

Type D4

Length (o.a.): 530' Breadth: 70'3""
Main engine: Doxford 6-cyl, opposed piston

	Completed	Tonnage Gross	Tonnage Deadweight	Notes
FLEETBANK	12.1972	11,452	16,634	(D & S)
CLOVERBANK	5.1973	11,452	16,633	(D & S)
BIRCHBANK	12.1973	11,452	16,635	(D & S)
BEAVERBANK	6.1974	11,452	16,901	(D & S)
CEDARBANK	6.1976	11,282	16,291	(Sund)
FIRBANK	11.1976	11,282	16,925	(Sund)
STREAMBANK	3.1977	11,281	16,925	(Sund)
RIVERBANK	5.1977	11,281	16,925	(Sund)
NESSBANK	9.1977	11,213	16,875	(Sund)
LAGANBANK	1.1978	11,213	16,875	(Sund)
CRESTBANK	4.1978	12,238	18,530	(Sund)
FENBANK	8.1978	12,238	18,400	(Sund)

Type D5

Length (o.a.): 531' Breadth: 75' 4"
Main engine: Doxford, 4-cyl, opposed piston

	Completed	Tonnage Gross	Tonnage Deadweight	Notes
ROACHBANK	1.1979	12,214	18,436	(Sund)
PIKEBANK	3.1979	12,214	18,436	(Sund)
DACEBANK	6.1979	12,214	18,501	(Sund)
RUDDBANK	6.1979	12,214	18,501	(Sund)
TROUTBANK	9.1979	12,214	18,501	(Sund)
TENCHBANK	11.1979	12,214	18,436	(Sund)

Vessels built by Swan, Hunter & Wigham Richardson.

Length (o.a.): 486' Breadth: 63'2"
Main engine Sulzer 5-cyl. twin stroke, single acting.

	Completed	Tonnage Gross	Tonnage Deadweight	Yard
SPEYBANK	6.1962	6,245*	10,387*	W
MARABANK	2.1963	6,249*	10,377*	W

Vessels built by Swan, Hunter Shipbuilders Ltd.

Length (o.a.): 530' Breadth: 74'0""
Main engine Doxford 6-cyl. opposed piston

	Completed	Gross	Deadweight	Yard
CORABANK	2.1973	11,405	15,216	S
MEADOWBANK	3.1973	11,405	15,461	W
FORTHBANK	11.1973	11,405	15,217	H
MORAYBANK	11.1973	11,405	15,216	S
IVYBANK	6.1974	11,405	15,216	S
CLYDEBANK	7.1974	11,405	15,460	H

Notes: Building Yard: H - Hebburn (Hawthorn, Leslie's yard)
S - South Shields (Readhead's yard),
W - Wallsend (Swan Hunter)
* Tonnage measured as completed as an open shelterdecker

Ruddbank had a remarkable and varied career spent entirely under the British flag. In 1983 she was the first of the 'Fishbank' class to be disposed of when sold to Lamport and Holt Line Ltd. Renamed *Romney*, she maintained their conventional service to South America - interrupted by a number of expeditions to the Falklands - until 1986. Then ostensibly acquired by an anonymous company having tenuous connections with the Hong Kong-based Wallem Shipmanagement Co., this was in fact no more than a complex exercise to conceal continuing ownership by the Vestey group. As *Lairg,* she now operated on their services between New Zealand and the west coast of North America. Vestey's involvement became a little more apparent in 1989 when Blue Star colours were adopted and she was renamed *Napier Star,* as which she is seen here at her namesake port. Two years later, a further sale saw the distinctive five pointed star funnel markings repainted in the dark green of Tamahine Shipping, when she joined the two other former Bank vessels in their fleet as *Tamapatcharee.* Weirs found themselves looking after their former charges again in 1993 when they were entrusted with the management of the Tamahine fleet. Sold yet again in 1995, the Hong Kong registration was retained by John McRink and Co. Ltd., who renamed her *Lady Rebecca.* The final sale came in 1998 after which, as *Global Mariner,* she was employed in a novel role by the International Transport Federation. Their worthy, but ultimately doomed, aim was to use the ship in a campaign against flag of convenience shipping and the exploitation of seafarers. Crewing problems reportedly beset the venture, but *Global Mariner* was to meet a far more climactic end to her career. On 2nd August 2000, now operating as a training ship, she was in collision with the container vessel *Atlantic Crusader* (7,366/1992) in the River Orinoco. Fully laden with a cargo of steel coils, she settled on the river bottom where she remains in a substantially submerged condition. [V. H. Young/P. Boot]

escape in the First World War when an enemy submarine fired a torpedo at her and missed while she was on passage in the North Sea on 4th August 1918.

The Northern Co-op sold the *Thrift* in December 1931 to R. Taylor and Sons Ltd., Dundee, and she was renamed *Berryden*. During that same year, the Northern Co-op had taken delivery of the second *Thrift* (648/1931) whose discharge berth at Aberdeen was frequently at Upper Quay right up until she made her last commercial voyage in August 1968. The *Berryden* frequently shipped bunker coal for the steam drifter fleets of Peterhead and Fraserburgh and the Moray Firth ports. During the Second World War, she carried supplies to Normandy in 1944, and in 1946 was sold to Maltese owners and renamed *San Giorg M.* Italian owners bought her in 1951 and in the following year she was broken up in Italy.

Across the dock, the elderly cargo steamer *Frankland* (728/1869) lies at Trinity Quay. This ship features in several photographs of the Upper Dock taken during this period and it is possible that she is laid-up. The *Frankland* was built by James Laing, Deptford, Sunderland, and was first registered in the ownership of Henry T. Morton, Biddick Hall, Durham. Her owners became Lambton Collieries Ltd., Sunderland in 1896 and she passed to Lambton and Hetton Collieries, Newcastle-upon-Tyne, in 1911. Although she had various registered owners, she was associated with Lambton Collieries throughout her long career which ended when she was broken up in 1914.

A small schooner is berthed in front of the Harbour Office, which was built between 1884 and 1886 on the site of the old Weigh House, and which has proved to be one of the most enduring landmarks at Aberdeen Harbour. An unidentified steamer lies at Regent Quay West whose wooden cargo transit shed was built in 1902 and survived until the 1960s.

It is worth mentioning that the last Aberdeen-owned collier, the *Ferryhill II* (199/1971), discharged her last coal cargo at Upper Quay in April 1978 before she was put up for sale. Today, commercial cargo ships rarely berth at Upper Quay, which now tends to accommodate various oil-related vessels. [Roy Fenton collection]

One can almost imagine hearing the clatter of hooves and the rumble of the carters' lorries over the granite setts in the atmospheric scene reproduced on this page, showing the corner of Upper and Trinity Quays some time between 1907 and 1911.

In the foreground, at Upper Quay, the coal dockers, locally known as 'blue badgers', are unloading coal from the elderly collier *Frederick Snowdon* (725gt), which was built by Bennie and Co., Middlesbrough, in 1866. She was the second ship owned by the Aberdeen Coal Co. and joined the firm's *Redhall* (884/1902) in June 1907. Sadly, she was fated to have a short career as an Aberdeen collier because she foundered during a storm off Cruden Bay, Aberdeenshire, on 17th January 1912 while nearing the end of a voyage from South Shields to Aberdeen. All 14 crew members went down with her.

Round the corner at Trinity Quay, the *Thrift* of the Northern Co-op is seen again discharging coal and berthed aft of the *Thrift* is the *Frankland*. [Aberdeen City Council, Arts and Recreation Department, PX-1-132-03]

ABERDEEN SCENES
Peter Myers

The view of the Upper Dock at Aberdeen on the opposite page dates from about 1910. In the foreground, at Upper Quay, two colliers are discharging their cargoes, and the scene demonstrates the antiquated and labour-intensive methods used to discharge coal at Aberdeen. The organisation at the quayside required to discharge a ton of coal consisted of seven men: two carriers, two lifters, two fillers and one winchman. The rate of discharge, using the iron tubs, was 15 to 18 tons per hour.

The elderly collier on the right has had pulley wheels attached to her mainmast's gaffs and her winches are being used to hoist the tubs out of her hold, whereupon the coal is emptied into sacks and then weighed. The sacks are being loaded on to eight-ton open box wagons of the Great North of Scotland Railway, which will be most likely hauled along the harbour lines to the company's Waterloo Goods Station which was adjacent to Waterloo Quay, beyond the right of the picture. The wagons owned by most of the Aberdeen coal merchants were, in fact, registered with the Caledonian Railway and the North British Railway. The former's Guild Street Goods Station was situated opposite Upper Quay.

The collier on the left is the *Thrift* (506/1904), owned by the Northern Co-operative Society Ltd., Aberdeen, and which was built by Aberdeen shipbuilder Hall, Russell and Co. Ltd. The *Thrift* had a narrow

In the upper photo steamships and a few sailing vessels congregate in the Victoria Dock, Aberdeen, viewed from the east end of Blaikies Quay in the early years of the 20th century. The only ship which can be identified with any certainty is the Royal Naval Reserve's drill ship HMS *Clyde*, a former sailing frigate which can be seen in the middle distance. She was relieved as drill ship at Aberdeen in 1904 by HM Sloop *Wild Swan* which was herself renamed *Clyde*. The Victoria Dock's mooring buoys were used frequently for laying-up ships until the early 1950s.

Beyond the ships moored in the middle of the dock can be glimpsed the two-storey cargo sheds at Regent Quay East, which were built between 1898 and 1900 and were particularly associated with the port's trades with North America, Hamburg and Rotterdam. The Regent Sheds survived until 1983 when they were demolished to make way for a modern cargo shed. *[Author's collection]*

There is plenty of activity at Blaikies Quay in the lower photograph which is dated 18th May 1914. Unfortunately the only vessel which can be identified is the Dutch tug *Roode Zee* (573/1908), the third from the left with her bow facing the camera. She was built by J. and K. Smit at Kinderdijk, and was owned by L. Smit and Co.'s Sleepdienst Ltd., Rotterdam, until 1933 when she was broken up at Hendrik ido Ambacht.

At the extreme left there are two steam drifters of which the outboard one is registered at Banff. The pristine state of her hull suggests she is a recent completion by a local shipyard, either Alexander Hall and Co. or the John Duthie Torry Shipbuilding Co., which both built steam drifters as well as steam trawlers.

Berthed forward of the drifters is a steam coaster with a long raised quarter-deck. Her decks are stacked high with timber which had quite likely arrived from Scandinavia. This berth at Blaikies Quay was a popular place for discharging timber imports as some of the local timber merchants had their premises on the quay.

Even as late as 1973, Blaikies Quay could still be a busy place handling a variety of cargoes. At the end of May that year one could find ten coasters berthed at the quay, discharging imports which included china clay, wood pulp, fertiliser and waste paper. *[Aberdeen City Council, Arts and Recreation Department, PX-1-131-35]*

This view of Blaikies Quay, looking west, shows the Sunderland-registered cargo steamer *Swaledale* with the Aberdeen-owned collier *Frederick Snowdon* berthed outboard of her. The latter's presence dates the picture as between 1907 and 1911.

The *Swaledale* (3,588/1897) was built as the *Ile De La Reunion* for Compagnie Havraise Peninsulaire de Navigation à Vapeur, of Le Havre, which traded between French ports and North Africa, Madagascar, Mozambique, Reunion and Mauritius. She was one of six ships built by Sir James Laing, Sunderland, for the firm between 1897 and 1903, and all

could accommodate 22 first and 32 second-class passengers. She was back in Laings' hands in 1903 as *Swaledale*, and it is quite likely they had taken her in part exchange for a new ship. She then had a variety of managers and owners under this name while still registered at Sunderland - including latterly Furness, Withy - before she was sold to Dutch owners in 1911 and renamed *Rijnsburg*. She was broken up at Alblasserdam in 1923.

One of Aberdeen Harbour Board's steam cranes, which were first introduced at the port in 1881, appears to be working the *Swaledale's*

forward hold, while another is at work a little farther along the quay. These cranes rendered yeoman service at Aberdeen, and continued in use until the end of the Second World War. The quay's granite setts were a characteristic feature of Aberdeen's harbour area and even today can still be found in some parts of the Granite City's dockland.

Bordering the quay, on the left of the picture, are the sheds of some of Aberdeen's timber importers. The elegant gas lampposts are another noteworthy feature of this quayside scene. *[Aberdeen City Council, Arts and Recreation Department, PX-1-156-14]*

125

the Harbour Office and close to the office of her owner, William Todd Moffatt, which was at 15 Regent Quay. The *Cairnie*'s funnel colours of yellow with a broad blue band, containing a white ball, and a black top resulted in Moffatt's coasters being nicknamed the 'Snowball Liners'. They were named after places in Aberdeenshire beginning with 'C' and ending with '-ie', including *Clunie, Collynie, Corennie* and *Crathie*.

The *Cairnie*, which was built by the Blyth Shipbuilding Co. Ltd, Blyth, appears to be discharging coal, which was her regular cargo and was often loaded at the smaller Forth ports such as Kennetpans in Clackmannanshire. Moffatt's sold the *Cairnie*, which was their last ship, to Matthew Taylor of Methil, Fife, in March 1912, and concentrated on their other interests which included ship and insurance broking, a forwarding agency, and being the Aberdeen agents for some of the leading passenger steamship lines of the period.

Captain J.D. Cheyne stayed on as master of the *Cairnie* under her new ownership, and she continued to ship coal to Aberdeen during the 1920s and 1930s. On 3rd April 1941 she was attacked and damaged by enemy aircraft off Tod Head while on passage from Methil to Holm, Orkney, with coal. She ran aground and was wrecked near the North Pier, Aberdeen. Her crew of seven was saved. *[Author's collection]*

the middle distance. The *St. Sunniva* was undoubtedly the most elegant steamship built at Aberdeen during the twentieth century. She was a larger version of the company's first *St. Sunniva* (864/1887), and her old-fashioned appearance, including her clipper stem, prompted the unkind remark that she was obsolete from the day she was launched. She served on the Leith/Aberdeen to Lerwick route until she was requisitioned in August 1939. The *St. Sunniva* was serving as a rescue ship with convoy ONS 158 when she disappeared without trace between 21st and 22nd January 1943. She was last seen on 21st January between Sable Island and Halifax, Nova Scotia, about 120 miles from her destination. Her sudden loss was presumed to have been caused by loss of stability due to severe icing. There were no survivors.

The ship berthed at the North Lock and close to the pair of sheerlegs derricks is the Renfrew-built steam suction dredger *Annie W. Lewis* which was first commissioned in July 1927 by the Aberdeen Harbour Commissioners. Over the next six years she dredged and deposited out at sea a total of 2½million tons of material which had been principally dredged from the navigation channel and the Tidal Harbour. Her work enabled large cargo ships, like the Greek tramp in the picture, to berth in the port. During this period the largest ship to enter the harbour, although she was not berthed at a quay, was the 488ft 2in-long *Rotenfels* (7,800/1927) which visited the port in 1929.

The *Annie W. Lewis* was withdrawn from service in April 1969 and was offered for sale along with the Harbour Board's *Grab Dredger No. 2*, which was built by Alexander Hall and Co. in 1931. Thereafter the Harbour Board employed dredging contractors.

On the opposite side of the Victoria Dock lies the Aberdeen Steam Navigation Co. Ltd.'s passenger and cargo steamer *Harlaw* (1,141/1911) which is berthed beside the firm's office at 87 Waterloo Quay. She had been acquired in 1929 from the General Steam Navigation Co. Ltd. of London, who had her built as the *Swift* by Ramage and Ferguson Ltd. of Leith. The *Harlaw* plied between Aberdeen and London and continued to do so during the war years when she was attacked by enemy aircraft on two occasions in 1941, but she sustained only minor damage. She maintained the London sailings after the war with the company's *Koolga* (1,110/1910) until she was withdrawn and sold to Chinese owners at the end of 1946. As the *Min Chih*, she had quite an eventful career in Far Eastern waters. In August 1953, she was seized by her Chinese Nationalist crew and sailed to Taiwan. She was later released, and in January 1955 she was involved in a collision but reached port safely. Two months later she was intercepted by a Chinese Nationalist warship but was later released. She was broken up at Hong Kong in 1963.

The taller of the two sheerlegs in the background were a familiar landmark at the harbour for many years. They had been erected in 1911 and were used for heavy lifts and for installing boilers and deck machinery when new ships were being fitted out at the North Lock. The sheerlegs, which had a lifting capacity of 100 tons, were dismantled in June 1975.

The Victoria Dock still presents a busy scene today, although most of the ships berthed at its quays are oil-related vessels, and for some the dock does not have quite the same fascinating appeal as 70 years ago. *[Courtesy of Aberdeen Journals Ltd.]*

The tartan-edged postcard reproduced right shows the long-lived steam coaster *Cairnie* (240/1891) lying at Regent Quay West, Aberdeen, beside

The fine, atmospheric photograph opposite, dating from the early 1930s, shows the east part of the Victoria Dock, Aberdeen, taken from above Blaikies Quay. Both the dock and the quay were built as a result of the Aberdeen Harbour Act of 1843. An interesting selection of ships can be seen, reflecting the port's involvement in the coastal, short-sea and ocean trades.

An unidentified Greek shelter-deck tramp steamer at Blaikies Quay dominates the other ships in the dock, and is discharging bagged grain, most probably loaded at one of the River Plate ports. Several such tramps visited the port between the wars, including (although this is not seen in her) the *Zannis L. Cambanis* (5,317/1920) which brought a big grain cargo from Rosario, Argentina in 1934 and was described as 'just scraping through the dock gates on the way to her berth at Blaikies Quay' after her 6,800-mile voyage.

The River Plate grain trade was quite active then and, as can be seen in the picture, the discharge of bagged grain was a slow and laborious business. Trestles and chutes have been set up to allow the sacks to slide down on to the waiting horse-drawn carts. The hessian sacks were likely to have been manufactured by the jute mills of Dundee, just 58 miles down the coast. A striking feature is the heavy reliance still placed on horses for quayside haulage, with no fewer than nine horse-drawn carts in view. One of the firms involved in quayside cartage at this period was the Shore Porters' Society, founded in 1498, and happily still in existence.

The only evidence of mechanised transport is a Sentinel steam wagon owned by Aberdeen haulage contractor John Davie. Horse-drawn carts could still be seen in the harbour area as late as 1968, while a Sentinel steam lorry of the Aberdeen Coal and Shipping Co. Ltd. was active until 1965.

The *Folda* (1,165/1920) of Christian Salvesen and Co., Leith is berthed aft of the Greek ship, and the stacks of timber on the quay suggest that this may have been the cargo she had brought from Norway. Aberdeen shipowner John Cook and Son had operated a cargo service between Aberdeen and Norway until 1928 when they sold the shipowning interest and the Norwegian service to Salvesen, with Cook's retaining an agency for the service in Aberdeen. The German occupation of Norway in 1940 brought the service to an end and it was not resumed in peacetime. The *Folda* had been built by J. Samuel White and Co. Ltd. of East Cowes, Isle of Wight, and was purchased from Alfred Rowland of Liverpool by Salvesen in April 1925, her previous names being *Aintree* and *Atlas*. She was employed on Salvesen's Norwegian service until 1940, when she was diverted to carrying supplies from Britain to France in aid of the British Expeditionary Force. Later in 1940, on 19th November, she was attacked by enemy aircraft in the southern North Sea and suffered bomb damage. Three lives were lost in the attack. The *Folda* exacted her revenge later when her gun crew shot down an attacking German bomber. Later in the war she carried supplies to Normandy in support of the Allied forces. In view of her age and her high coal consumption, Salvesen withdrew the *Folda* from service in 1956 and she was sold for demolition.

An unidentified steam coaster is berthed ahead of the *Folda*. Lying at the easternmost end of Blaikies Quay is the *St. Sunniva* (1,368/1931) of the North of Scotland, Orkney and Shetland Steam Navigation Co. Ltd., Aberdeen, and whose presence helps to date the picture. She was built by Hall, Russell and Co. Ltd., whose yard at Footdee, and the neighbouring yard of Alexander Hall and Co. Ltd., can be seen in

EVERY PICTURE TELLS A STORY

In accordance with wartime practice, the hull of this vessel carries no name, but the name pennant at the fore identifies her as *Supremity*. Indeed, even without this she can be easily identified: a large vessel flying F.T. Everard's houseflag and with a variant on their funnel colours, obviously on trials in the Humber during wartime could only be this motorship, launched at Goole on 26th February 1944. The date of the photograph is undoubtedly October 1944 - *Supremity* was registered in Everard's ownership in London on 21st October 1944.

A small mystery surrounds this ship. Much merchant ship production during the Second World War was of standard vessels for Government account. Owners could and did place their own orders, but these were almost invariably to existing designs. *Supremity* was a novel design, being - as her names suggests - much larger than anything previously built for their Greenhithe-based owners. She had a length of 270 feet and a gross tonnage of 2,074. Her nearest relative was the 1947-built *Superiority*, which was one foot deeper, increasing her gross tonnage to 2,145. So why were Everards allowed to build *Supremity*?

Ken Garrett, author of *Everard of Greenhithe*, suggests that a clue might lie in her machinery. This came from the Everard-owned Newbury Diesel Co. Ltd., and was the first of the 6-cylinder 'P' type two-stroke diesels which had been under development since 1942. Did one of the Everard family persuade the Ministry of War Transport to let them order the ship as a floating test bed? They may have used the argument that it would be a waste of the time, effort and material put into the development work if the engine could not be put into a ship.

Another interesting feature is the Everard funnel, or at least a variant on it, with no yellow above the red and white band. This may have been painted up purely for the trials which would be conducted within the Humber. The funnel would be painted over in grey when she went out to face the wartime dangers, as the threats from U-boats and E-boats were by no means over at this late stage of the war. *Supremity* was well armed with guns on each bridge wing and more on the poop. Ken notes that her name would have been displayed on a board on the side of the deckhouse. This would have been hinged longitudinally and at sea the top half would be flapped down to make her incognito.

The shot was probably taken by Norman Burnitt, who had a shop in Mariner Street, Goole and did most of the photography for Goole ship trials.

Supremity gave Everards twenty years' service, being sold in May 1964 to John Capralos of Piraeus to become *Kapa*, his only ship. Two years later she passed to Karmiris Brothers, also of Piraeus, to become *Irene K*, and after a later career spent largely in the Mediterranean she was sold to breakers at Skaramanga late in 1973.